The Charismatic Advisor™

Becoming a *source of strength* in the lives of your clients

Robert Brooks, Ph.D., and David Richman

The examples and discussions throughout this book revolve around the financial advisory relationship, but we believe that the principles identified are directly applicable as well to all those in the position of delivering advice to others. Though most of the stories represent actual advisors, some are composites. All scenarios represent the real-life situations of financial advisors and their clients.

We dedicate this book to the many advisors who have inspired us in our quest to identify the attributes of the Charismatic Advisor. Without their help, this book would not have been possible.

———————

To my wife Marilyn; my sons and daughters-in-law, Rich and Cybèle, Doug and Suzanne; and my grandchildren, Maya, Teddy, Sophie, and Lyla, for your ongoing love and support and for the joy you always provide. I hope that your journeys through life will be in the presence of people from whom you gather strength and, in turn, you will be a source of strength for others.

— Bob

———————

In honor of
Irwin L. Kipness *("Big Irv")*
January 7, 1942 — October 22, 2009

Our beloved uncle, whose genuine warmth and authenticity had an indelible impact on so many and whose memory will forever remain a source of strength to my wife Faigie; our children, Alanna, Jason, and Ryan; and me.

— David

Table of Contents

Introduction

As an advisor do you ever wonder . . .
- Is my own mindset or perspective holding me back from greater success?
- Do my clients see me as an essential resource in providing financial security in their lives?
- Are there skills I can develop and maintain so my clients feel an increasing sense of trust and loyalty between us?
- If clients see me as a source of strength, are they likely to refer other people to me without my asking?
- How do I communicate more effectively to motivate both current clients and prospective clients to modify the status quo when it is actually hindering their financial security?
- How do I respond to clients who seem resistant to my recommendations?
- What steps can I take to ensure my team is functioning as smoothly as possible?

Insights on these and similar questions will be found in this book, a collaboration between a clinical psychologist and an expert in the financial services field. What led Bob and David to collaborate and use the term "Charismatic Advisor"?

Background

When Bob first began his career as a clinical psychologist more than forty years ago, the dominant focus in his field was examining what was wrong with people. Courses in his undergraduate and graduate studies had such titles as "Abnormal Psychology," "Psychopathology of Childhood," and "Psychopathology of Adolescence." Researchers and clinicians directed little if any attention or energy to identifying or utilizing the strengths of individuals.

In the mid-1970s Bob became increasingly interested in understanding those factors that help people overcome or bounce back from adversity and become resilient. He began to ask why some children could rise from poverty, racism, emotional or physical abuse, or constant failure in school to lead more successful lives as

1

adults—success measured not simply by one's income level but rather by such variables as contentment in interpersonal relationships, marriages, and work.

Psychologists began to conduct studies to identify factors that help people to be resilient. Within the past ten to fifteen years, especially with the emergence of "positive psychology" as a dominant movement in the field of psychology, these studies have multiplied at a seemingly exponential rate.

A number of studies involved researchers interviewing adults who had overcome great hardship. They asked, "What do you think was one of the most important things in your childhood or adolescence that helped you to be more optimistic and successful, especially given all that you faced as a child?" In study after study the first answer was the same; namely, that they could recall at least one person who believed in and stood by them. These studies highlighted the power of one adult to change a child's life forever.

In an article written in 1988, the late psychologist Dr. Julius Segal, one of Bob's heroes in the study of resilience, referred to this type of person as a "charismatic adult." Bob found Segal's definition of such an adult to be poetic: "an adult from whom a child or adolescent gathers strength."

In his writings and workshops, Bob began to ask parents, "When you put your kids to bed at night do you ask, 'Have my children gathered strength from me today? Have I been a charismatic adult in their lives?'" He posed similar questions for teachers, mental health professionals, and other caregivers, encouraging them to think about the impact they were having on the children in their lives.

To assist parents and others to reflect upon the role of a charismatic adult, Bob asked the following questions of participants at his workshops:

- Who were two or three charismatic adults in your life when you were a child or an adolescent?
- What did these people specifically say or do to prompt you to see them as your charismatic adults?
- Are you saying or doing similar things with your own children?

- Would your children consider you a charismatic adult in their lives?

His participants told Bob that these questions prompted much thought, and it was not unusual for them to tell him, "I want to be a charismatic adult. What do I say or do to become one?" In his writings, especially with his colleague Dr. Sam Goldstein, Bob attempted to identify specific actions parents and others could take to become charismatic adults in the lives of children.

In focusing on the ways in which we can help youngsters be more resilient, Bob was constantly asked by adults, "Can we help kids be resilient if we ourselves are feeling stressed and pessimistic?" His answer was that it definitely is more difficult to assume the role of a charismatic adult if the adult is not coping very effectively with life's challenges. These questions also served as a catalyst for Bob to expand his work and writings about resilience into the adult years.

Thus, when a woman in one of his workshops asked the thought-provoking question, "Do we, as adults, need charismatic adults in our lives?" Bob was not surprised. He responded by commenting, "Unless we've decided to be hermits, we all need charismatic adults in our lives at any age. We all need people from whom we gather support and strength."

Paralleling the questions he posed about kids, Bob encouraged his audiences to think about who their past and present charismatic adults were and for whom they serve as charismatic adults.

In early 2007 David asked Bob to speak at an evening event at a private school in Rhode Island in support of a financial advisory team. When David witnessed the audience's deep emotional reaction to the concept of the charismatic adult, it hit him:

What financial advisor wouldn't love to be seen as the charismatic adult in the lives of his or her clients? To be held in the lofty position in the minds and hearts of clients as a person from whom they gather strength? Wouldn't this lead to the ultimate higher calling for advisors, creating advisor relationships for life and a consistent and endless stream of quality referrals?

David shared his thoughts with Bob about applying the concept of the charismatic adult to the role of the financial advisor. Bob was immediately intrigued, and from this initial phone conversation a thoughtful, exciting collaboration was born, leading to the writing of this book and the delivery of workshops around the country.

Bob is a highly sought-after speaker on topics of resilience, motivation, and self-esteem. David has been ensconced in the financial services world his entire thirty-year career, is an inspirational speaker, and has evolved into a coach for many of the nation's top financial advisors and aspiring advisors alike. His experience has led him to conclude that the nation's best advisors effectively position themselves with clients at the intersection where life and money meet.

The Charismatic Advisor has been developed by dealing with another intersection; that is, the intersection where the mind of a clinical psychologist meets that of an expert of the financial advisory experience.

A Note from the Authors

We are often asked, "Can we really teach someone to become a Charismatic Advisor?" We believe it is a skill set that can indeed be taught. In our research on this topic, we have interviewed many advisors whom we believe exemplify the characteristics of the Charismatic Advisor. Where appropriate, we share some of their insights and our observations.

In our collaboration we have also received such questions as these: "Are financial advisors really prepared to take on this responsibility?" "Do we have the training to play this kind of role?" to which we respond that we believe financial advisors can serve this role, especially if they understand the skills involved in being a Charismatic Advisor and are willing to work on strengthening these skills. So much of life's dreams and worries relate to money. If not the financial advisor, who else will step into this role?

And as we will emphasize, the Charismatic Advisor lives in *conversations*:

- Conversations advisors have with clients and prospects
- Conversations clients have with friends and family about the advisor when he or she is not in the room

- Conversations advisors have with their team members
- Conversations advisors have with themselves

We would now like to continue our conversation, with the goal of helping you become a Charismatic Advisor — an advisor from whom clients gather strength. We'll begin with the all-important discussion of mindsets, but first, let's reflect on the questions below:

Reflections

Do you have a doctor you brag about?

Perhaps you have a family doctor you think is amazing. Chances are you tell your friends about her when the topic of health or doctors comes up in conversation. Often those friends will get a sense of how competent she is, but you probably value her most for all the interest she takes in your life. Recently, one of Connecticut's most sought-after doctors told David, "When I knock on the examination room and enter, I leave myself behind." Her statement captured the importance she places on focusing exclusively on the patient. In so doing, she ensures that her patients are very likely to refer others to her.

We will discuss the topic of referrals in Chapter 9. For the moment, we ask you to reflect on the following thought: wouldn't it be bizarre if this doctor ended her examinations by asking, "So . . . do you have some friends who might like to consider my help?" The skills of a great doctor and great advisors have strong similarities and are embodied in the Charismatic Advisor.

Neither great doctors nor great advisors need to ask patients or clients for referrals. Because they are a source of significant strength to the lives they touch, they get referrals without having to ask for them.

CHAPTER 1

The Power of Mindsets

Imagine for a moment you are meeting two prospective clients, Cindy and Art Lansing, for the first time. Even before he is seated, Art says, "I'm not certain we need a financial advisor. I think I can handle things pretty well myself, but Cindy seems to think we could benefit from having an advisor."

Cindy, with a sense of exasperation in her voice, responds, "Art always likes to do things by himself. He thinks I'm criticizing his financial judgment by consulting an advisor. I've tried to tell him that I think having another viewpoint can help our finances. A good friend recommended you."

Art glances at his wife with a skeptical look on his face. He turns to you and says, "Well, I'm here, so I'll listen to your opinions. But before we begin, how much do you charge? When I asked Cindy, she said she couldn't remember. Also, a friend of mine saw a financial advisor, and he said he ended up losing a lot of money in his portfolio. Do most of your clients make money with your advice?"

Think about what feelings might be triggered by Art's comments. Reflect upon your understanding of Art's behavior. Whether we realize it or not, we continually make assumptions about ourselves and other people. Often we accept these assumptions as the truth, not recognizing that there may be reasons for people's behavior that we're not aware of. Very importantly, the perceptions we harbor of ourselves and others play a major role in determining the actions we take in countless situations.

For example, the words we use to evaluate ourselves as a financial advisor (or husband, wife, father, mother, manager, employee) will greatly influence how effectively we handle that role. Psychologists have found that our sense of self-efficacy determines, to a great extent, our success in particular situations. The more confident we feel, the more likely the outcome of our actions will be positive. If an advisor sitting with Art is insecure about his ability to handle challenging clients, the greater is the probability

7

that Art's comments will trigger further doubts. The advisor might think, "Why did I agree to meet with these prospects? I bet Art won't agree to work with me, and even if he does he will be a pain, always ready to criticize me. I hope he ends up walking out." Such thoughts will find expression both verbally and non-verbally in the insecure, ineffective ways in which the advisor responds.

In contrast, an advisor who views herself as more competent and self-assured might think, "Art asks challenging questions, but I'm glad he does. I'd rather have his concerns right out in the open so I can address them, rather than having them go unmentioned." This advisor, rather than being intimidated by Art's demeanor, adopts a problem-solving approach for developing a working relationship with her seemingly reluctant prospect.

If the first advisor were asked to describe Art, his words might have a more negative tone, such as argumentative, resistant, or angry. The second advisor might use such descriptions as out in the open, forthright, direct, and honest.

If questioned, both advisors might perceive their descriptions of Art as capturing the truth, but they both should recognize that these so-called truths are based, in part, on their subjective perceptions. And these perceptions will then determine the ways in which they each interact with Art.

In the numerous workshops we have conducted discussing this topic with advisors from across the industry, we have noted that a disproportionate number have voiced very negative visceral responses to Art. As we will explore in Chapter 3, such visceral responses to a client or prospect who's perceived as difficult can present considerable challenges for advisors. Even if advisors don't directly express such negative emotions, it is hard to hide these feelings from clients and prospects.

The emergence of negative feelings in advisors is even more acute during or in the aftermath of difficult market environments. Faced with significant losses to their portfolios, many prospects and clients are filled with anxiety; many believe they have been betrayed perhaps by you, another advisor, a particular firm, or maybe the entire financial system. Perhaps they aren't certain who has betrayed them, but it has led to an enormous level of skepticism about the markets, investing, and the fundamental tenets of asset allocation and diversification.

The Mindsets of Charismatic Advisors

In our day-to-day interactions with others, we constantly make assumptions and develop expectations. In this book we refer to these assumptions and expectations as "mindsets." In reflecting upon this concept, let's consider the following questions:
- What is the mindset of financial advisors who are extremely successful in cultivating client relationships?
- What assumptions do these advisors make about themselves and their clients that contribute to an effective working relationship?
- What is the mindset of a Charismatic Advisor; that is, an advisor from whom clients gather strength?

What follows is an overview of some of the key characteristics of the mindset of Charismatic Advisors, all of which will be elaborated upon in subsequent chapters. As you read these characteristics, reflect upon the degree to which you subscribe to or follow each of them.

Developing and sustaining a caring relationship. Clients and prospects want to feel we genuinely care about them. In education there is a saying that "students don't care what you know until they first know you care." This statement can be transferred to the world of the financial advisor; clients and prospects won't care what you know until you show them that you care.

What would your clients say if they were asked how they know you are really interested in them as people, not just clients? You might find your own answers if you think about what the professionals you deal with, such as your doctor or your lawyer, do to let you know that they genuinely care about you. By the same token you can consider what diminishes the belief that someone regards you as a real person.

An advisor whom we admire greatly is John Rafal, who runs Essex Financial Services in Connecticut. *Barron's* considers him to be one of the country's top 100 advisors year in and year out. Yes, John manages over $2 billion, but that's not how John and his clients measure his success. John's clients are true zealots. Why? When you speak to his clients, you find that they tend to talk about what John did for their son-in-law or their granddaughter. John considers it all "the little things you do to help people." Yet none of his clients sees his acts and deeds as "little things." They see his interest and actions as evidence of someone who actually cares about them.

Nurturing trust. The concept of caring is inextricably interwoven with another significant feature of an effective relationship; namely, trust. The same kinds of questions raised about caring apply to trust:

- What is trust, and what does trust involve?
- How do I nurture a feeling of trust in my clients?
- Who are the people in my life whom I trust? What do they say or do that reinforces this sense of trust?

Taking responsibility for changing the situation. If something is not working effectively in a relationship with a client, we must not blame ourselves or our clients but rather should ask, "What can I do differently to change the situation?" This belief serves as a basic foundation of resilience. In reality, since we have control over only one person in our lives — ourselves — it is empowering to examine what we can do differently. If we wait for the other person to change first, we may wait forever.

When faced with a prospective client such as Art, a Charismatic Advisor considers the steps necessary to respond effectively to Art's hesitancy to engage a financial advisor, rather than expect that Art will magically change his outlook. A Charismatic Advisor also recognizes that if he comes across as siding with Cindy, he is likely to contribute to Art's perception that he is being outnumbered, which may lead Art to become more defensive.

Presenting new ideas in thoughtful ways. You will find that most clients and prospects are open to change if new ideas are presented in ways that lessen their defensiveness and increase their receptiveness. Should you perceive a client's or prospect's resistance or anger as fixed and not open to modification, it will be easy to give up on that client or prospect or become frustrated or angry in return. Power struggles may ensue that result in negative outcomes. However, if you believe that most people are willing to consider a different idea or perspective, then you as the advisor will be more willing to change your approach, and the client, in turn, may be more receptive to modifying his view. The question is how best to present new ideas so the client is willing to reflect upon rather than quickly reject them.

Viewing challenging situations as opportunities to deliver alternatives. Especially during turbulent financial times, it's easy to become overwhelmed with stress and anxiety. Charismatic Advisors view turbulent times as opportunities to reevaluate the situation, to change short- and long-term goals and strategies, and to remain calm. An advisor can voice concern about market situations, but if his clients perceive their advisor's concern as stress, it will only add to their sense of panic. Charismatic Advisors adopt the view that problems must be met with problem solving rather than "catastrophic thinking" and resigned behavior. In adhering to a problem-solving approach, Charismatic Advisors don't minimize the turbulent times — they acknowledge the situation but present realistic, credible options for managing the crisis.

Appreciating that clients desire a collaborative relationship. While the word "advisor" is part of our title and our clients expect us to offer advice, it is important for us to recognize that each person wants to be heard. If clients feel we are not considering their point of view or do not understand their perspective, they are less likely to work collaboratively. Even with clients who might declare, "Just tell me what to do; you're the expert," we must be cautious in summarily telling them what to do. As advisors we must discover ways to nurture collaboration and help clients feel they are actively involved in decisions. We must constantly seek their feedback and make certain they understand any data we present.

Another advisor whom we admire is Lori Van Dusan, who runs a national consulting practice from Pittsford, New York. Like John Rafal, Lori is frequently cited by *Barron's* as being among the nation's best advisors. She oversees the management of more than $4 billion in assets, much of which is run for endowments and foundations. Lori is extremely bright and candid. When asked, "How can you be opinionated yet foster a spirit of collaboration, especially when dealing with investment boards?" her response was quite telling: "It's about being decisive in your opinions, yet collaborative in your approach." Lori is masterful in her ability to orchestrate a committee's consensus, while also being able to maintain her role as expert consultant with dignity and respect.

Practicing empathy. A basic skill that must be applied to enrich any relationship is empathy; that is, the ability to place yourself in the shoes of others and see the world through their eyes. Empathy is sometimes confused with sympathy, but they differ. Sympathy implies feeling sorry for someone, while empathy is associated with understanding the other person's perspective. Noted psychologist Dr. Daniel Goleman has observed that empathy is a key feature of emotional intelligence (EQ) and that EQ plays a major role in success and happiness in both our personal and professional lives.

Charismatic Advisors are proficient in applying empathy in their interpersonal relationships. To strengthen empathy, you might wish to reflect upon these questions:

- What words would I hope my clients use to describe me?
- What have I said or done in the past few months to make it likely that they would use these words?
- What words would they actually use?
- How do I know what words they would actually use? How do I obtain feedback from them?
- What must I do so the words they actually use are the same words I *hope* they use?

Using empathic communication and validation. How would you have responded to Art's reservations about consulting with a financial advisor? Empathic communication, which is rooted in empathy, can be very helpful. Be guided by these questions:

- In everything I say and do with clients and prospects, what do I hope to accomplish?
- Am I communicating to clients and prospects in such a way that they are likely to listen to my message and want to work with me?
- Do my communications create a "motivating environment"; that is, an environment characterized by trust, empathy, and cooperation?

We will discuss in detail the concept of a "motivating environment" in Chapter 6. In the situation we described with Art, an advisor could easily become annoyed and question whether he or she wants Art as a client. However, if your goal is to create a "motivating environment" in which Art will want to work with you, you must practice empathy and show Art that his concerns are valid. Validation doesn't mean you necessarily agree with another person's views but rather that you are striving to understand the meaning and intent of his message.

For example, when Art asserts that he thinks he can handle finances on his own and questions how much you charge, then asks if most of your clients make money, a validating response might be, "The questions you're raising are very important, and it's obvious that you've thought a lot about the role of a financial advisor. I will attempt to answer all your questions, and I want to explain to you as clearly as possible the role I can play as your advisor. Then you'll be in a better position to decide whether you need a financial advisor and, if you do, whether you want to retain me in that capacity. If both of you feel I can be of assistance, then it's important to determine whether there is a fit between what you might be looking for in an advisor and what I represent. Beyond technical issues, we should determine whether we have the right chemistry. If not, that doesn't mean there is something wrong with you or me. It just means we may not be a good fit. Does that make sense?"

While the effectiveness of this kind of response on the part of an advisor may seem obvious, when we are feeling challenged, we may inadvertently present a defensive rather than a collaborative manner.

Understanding a client's main ways of coping. If we are to assume the role of a Charismatic Advisor, we must appreciate that we and our clients apply different forms of coping when facing challenges. As we will discuss in Chapter 7, some strategies for coping are effective, resulting in personal growth as we each successfully face the challenging situations that confront us. Unfortunately, other strategies are self-defeating and serve only to exacerbate the situation (for example, clients who are so upset with their finances that they refuse to review their financial statements or they scream at their advisor are not coping effectively). Charismatic Advisors appreciate that coping strategies are "recruited" as a protective shield. If managed with empathy and caring, clients are more likely to give up counterproductive strategies and engage us in a more cooperative manner.

A Comment from the Audience

Earlier, we highlighted one feature of the mindset of a Charismatic Advisor as the belief that challenging situations afford opportunities for change rather than increased stress. If, as advisors, we feel anxious, we are likely to convey an image of worry and uncertainty to our clients. Such an image will compromise our ability to work effectively and collaboratively with them. What client wants to entrust his portfolio to an advisor who does not demonstrate realistic optimism?

At the end of an all-day workshop given by Bob on the power of resilience, a woman in the audience raised her hand and commented, "I love your ideas, but I'm too stressed out to use them." While there was a degree of levity in her voice, it was overshadowed by the serious tone of her comment. She voiced what many have experienced; namely, that if we are stressed and exhausted, we are less likely to take steps that may improve the situation, especially if we harbor doubts that things can get better.

If we don't manage our own stress effectively, we will never attain the status of a Charismatic Advisor. Our next chapter specifically examines what we can do to become more stress hardy.

Reflections

Have you ever had a prospective client like Art? What was your initial reaction? Did you have some negative feelings? How did you respond? Having read this first chapter, might you respond differently if you face such a prospect again?

CHAPTER 2

Becoming Stress Hardy, Not Stressed Out

Andrew and Staci work at the same financial advisory firm. Both are conscientious, dedicated and responsive to their clients. They enjoy their work and feel fortunate to have entered a field that has brought such satisfaction as well as comfortable styles of living.

These positive feelings and thoughts were evident when the market was going up; even dips in the market were seen as temporary hiccups and not worthy of great concern. Andrew and Staci exuded an air of confidence that seemed unshakable, and they enjoyed their personal lives with their spouses and children. However, ominous events appeared that soon would test their confidence and stress levels. The market fell precipitously and what were once deemed to be "safe" investments were subject to rapid decline. Understandably, both Andrew and Staci were shaken by this unexpected situation, but their mindsets and subsequent responses were strikingly different.

Andrew began to experience moments of panic, reflected in both physical and emotional symptoms. He had headaches, heart palpitations, and difficulty sleeping. His confidence disappeared as he reflected on the assets he felt he had lost for his clients. His seemingly secure foundation began to fall like crumbling rock. He became obsessed with watching CNBC, his stomach churning with each downturn in the market numbers. Having his eyes glued to the television left little time to return phone calls to his clients or initiate contact with them. He was convinced that each time he spoke with a client, that client was thinking, "Andrew is a lousy financial advisor who has lost a lot of my money."

Not surprisingly, Andrew's anxiety, despondency, and irritability impacted his relationship with his wife and two young children. He was less patient with his children and even when he was with them, he was preoccupied with work. At one point Andrew's wife commented that she was aware of the pressure he was feeling at work but thought it was important for him to be more involved with their kids. He angrily retorted, "Stop criticizing me.

I'm trying to earn a living to support you and the kids, and you keep telling me I should be a better father. You probably think I should be a better husband, too!"

Andrew's self-esteem plummeted. He questioned whether he should have ever gone into a career in the financial world. He fell prey to a victim's mentality, constantly asking, "Why did this have to happen to me?" He failed to consider that his situation was not unique but was the reality for countless advisors and clients around the world. His eating habits suffered, and his exercise diminished. He gained weight and felt like even more of a failure when he realized how tight his clothes had become.

Staci was also upset by the rapid downturn in the market but displayed ways of coping that were in marked contrast to those of Andrew. She felt few, if any, advisors could have foreseen the deterioration of the economy. Rather than blame herself or avoid her clients, she assumed a proactive approach.

Staci sent an e-mail to each of her clients. In addressing the current state of the economy, she offered a realistic appraisal that was free of a fatalistic attitude. At the beginning of the letter, she noted that the assets in all of her clients' portfolios had diminished and acknowledged how scary and upsetting that could be. She added that a natural urge would be to transfer all of one's portfolio to cash but reminded her clients that a great deal of thought had gone into the allocation in their portfolios. However, rather than simply encourage the status quo, she suggested to her clients that this was a good time to meet and reassess their portfolios and consider possible changes in a thoughtful manner.

Staci recognized that during these pressured times it was important that she take care of herself. She made certain that she continued her regular regimen of exercise and diet and that she spend time with her two preschool daughters, including reading to them each night before putting them to bed. Although she brought some work home, she kept it to a minimum so she didn't sacrifice time with her husband. After one especially brutal day in the market, her husband asked her if she had regrets about being a financial advisor. She smiled and said, "It's a lot easier being an advisor when portfolios are going up, but even in these difficult times I feel that I made the right professional choice. I feel I can still make a positive difference in the lives of my clients."

Staci had prepared her clients for a possible downturn in the market. As portfolios were going up and Staci's clients complimented her abilities as a financial advisor, she told them she was delighted by how well their assets were doing. She cautioned, however, that based on historical patterns there were likely to be times when portfolios decreased in value. She emphasized that she hoped those times would be brief in duration, adding that when they occurred she would be there to work closely with her clients to reassess their portfolios. She told her husband, "I never thought we would see the financial crisis that exists today, but I think my clients feel assured that I'm here for them." And throughout the crisis she attempted to maintain a balanced life.

The Impact of Stress on Our Lives

Andrew and Staci — two people with similar jobs but strikingly different outlooks. One was obviously more stressed than the other. But why? In what ways do they differ? The more we understand what contributes to Staci's positive mindset or attitude, the more the Andrews of the world will be able to work on improving their negative mindset. A financial advisor who possesses a positive outlook will not only be better equipped to handle turbulent times but will be able to help her clients do the same.

Adopting Stress Hardiness

As Bob and his colleague, Dr. Sam Goldstein, wrote in their book *The Power of Resilience: Achieving Balance, Confidence, and Personal Strength in Your Life*, assessing the impact stress has on all aspects of our lives invites these questions:

- What are the factors that help people respond to difficult situations in a less stressed manner?
- Do people who are less stressed see the world and themselves differently from those who are more vulnerable to stress? If so, what are these differences, and can they be learned?

- In what ways do less stressed people respond to events that distinguish them from their more stressed counterparts?

Reflect how you might answer these questions in relation to Andrew and Staci. Our inborn temperament plays a role in how effectively we cope with pressure; that is, research indicates that from birth some individuals are predisposed to experiencing stress more intensely than others. However, psychologists also know that inborn temperament is not the sole determinant of one's level of stress; many life experiences, including our interactions with others as children and adults, contribute to our perceptions and reactions to challenging situations.

Andrew and Staci displayed markedly contrasting reactions to the downward economic spiral. The research of psychologist Dr. Suzanne Kobasa and her colleagues offers information not only for understanding their different reactions but also guidelines for becoming less stressed and more resilient. Kobasa identified three characteristics of what she called the *stress-hardy personality*. Individuals who possess these characteristics experience and respond to seemingly stressful events in a more adaptive, constructive way than those who are limited in these characteristics.

Given our emphasis on the concept of mindsets, we prefer to refer to a stress-hardy *mindset*. Also, the word *mindset* seems more associated with the possibility of change than that of *personality*, which is often interpreted as fixed and resistant to modification. The word *mindset* represents our belief that we all have the capacity to make changes in our thinking and actions to be more stress hardy.

The three characteristics of a stress-hardy mindset are commitment, challenge, and control — the "3 Cs." As we describe them, ask yourself:

- Do I strive to lead a stress-hardy life, even in the face of adversity?
- Do I practice each component in my daily life?
- If not, what steps must I take to assume this mindset and lead a more stress-hardy, resilient lifestyle?

Commitment. Kobasa defined *commitment* as being involved with, rather than alienated from, the many aspects of life. When commitment is present, we possess a sense of purpose that tells us why we are doing what we are doing. We are directed by a vision that provides passion and meaning to our lives and diminishes the impact of stress. In essence, even in troubling times we have a reason for waking up each morning and confronting life's challenges. Commitment is not confined to a single arena but is evident in our personal relationships, in our work, in our charitable activities, in causes we adopt, and in our religious or spiritual practices. It is difficult to lead a stress-hardy life devoid of purpose.

Consider the following questions:
- What are two or three activities that give meaning and purpose to my life?
- What energizes me?
- Do the main activities in which I engage give meaning to my life?
- Do I derive satisfaction from each of these activities?
- Why did I enter the profession I did?

As you reflect on these questions, it might be helpful to provide a couple of examples of *commitment* and *purpose*. Psychologist Julius Segal, who introduced the notion of "charismatic adult," observed that we are better able to deal with life's struggles if we give "purpose to our pain." He emphasized that altruism, an unselfish desire to help others, can minimize stress by providing meaning to actions.

Segal described the response of Eileen Stevens to the death of her twenty-year-old son, who died as a consequence of a college fraternity incident in which he was instructed to drink large amounts of liquor. Stevens noted that "tragedy has a way of getting priorities in order," and she founded the Committee to Halt Useless College Killings (CHUCK). She began to devote her time to speaking with and writing to hundreds of fraternities across the country and encouraging many states to pass laws that posed limits on dangerous hazing activities.

Stevens emphasized, "I travel, I speak, I share information. . . . I've channeled my grief in a positive direction."

Perhaps one of the most poignant and vivid examples of the power of commitment or purpose was captured in the experiences of a Holocaust survivor, the renowned Austrian psychiatrist, Dr.

The Charismatic Advisor

Viktor Frankl, developer of a form of psychotherapy known as *logotherapy,* or *meaning therapy.* In his book *Man's Search for Meaning,* Frankl describes a moment while imprisoned in a concentration camp when his will to live had all but evaporated. He realized that if he were to survive, he must discover some purpose to his life even within the death camp, some force that would permit him to go on.

But what could he call upon? The purpose he found was to imagine himself lecturing after the war about what had transpired in the concentration camps, to help others understand and appreciate what he and many millions had experienced. Frankl confronted unfathomable sadness, pain, and resignation through the act of articulating a goal and an image that served to provide meaning to his life. Given the horrors and mass murders in the concentration camps, Frankl could not have predicted he would survive. What he knew was that as long as he was alive, he could draw strength from an image of his lecturing in the future. For Frankl the image was to become a reality.

We are not suggesting that what Andrew, Staci, and most financial advisors faced at the depth of this past bear market is anywhere near the intense anguish and pain of the loss of one's child or of the horrific experiences of the concentration camps. However, the stories of Eileen Stevens and Victor Frankl enlighten us with information that can help us become less stressed.

Let's examine Andrew's and Staci's situations in terms of the concepts of commitment and purpose. If we had asked them prior to the market's taking a tumble what their main priorities in life were, they both would have listed their marriages, their children, their health, and their job responsibilities. However, when the tough times arrived, Staci kept her equilibrium by not losing sight of these priorities, since they added meaning to and enriched her life. Although it was not always easy, she made certain she spent uninterrupted time with her daughters and her husband. She also adhered to a sensible diet and engaged in regular exercise to ensure that her health did not deteriorate; she knew that exercise was an effective antidote to stress.

When Staci's husband asked her if she regretted becoming a financial advisor, she didn't minimize the current struggles, but she believed that her career choice was the right one and that it provided her with an opportunity to enrich the lives of her clients. This attitude was reflected in her reaching out to clients to deal with their questions and ease their anxieties.

Maintaining the sense of balance and purpose displayed by Staci is not easily accomplished. However, by observing Andrew's reactions we can see what happens when a sense of purpose begins to dissipate. The turmoil of the economy was quickly paralleled by Andrew's inner turmoil. He lost faith in his ability as an advisor and questioned if he should have entered the profession. His self-doubt and insecurities grew rapidly, prompting him to withdraw from contact with his clients, an action that served only to add to his feelings of failure.

His declining sense of purpose at work soon found its way to his personal life. Rather than find comfort and meaning in his relationship with his wife and children, he allowed these relationships to be injected with anger and distance. His diet, exercise, and physical health deteriorated. When balance and purpose are absent in a person's life, emotional and physical well-being can fall apart surprisingly quickly.

All of the advisors whom we know who best exemplify the attributes of Charismatic Advisor have a profound dimension to their sense of "commitment." Augie Cenname is such an advisor. Augie is one of the country's most successful advisors and consistently is among the top advisors cited in *Barron's* Top 100 list. A number of years ago Augie had a true near-death experience. When the police arrived on the scene, they were astonished that someone could make it out alive from this horrific car accident.

After the accident, Augie asked himself: "How do I want my life to be viewed?" He chose to focus on "acute awareness" as a way to make certain he completely lives in the moment. This directly translates into not only the *way* he has conversations with his clients but what he has conversations *about*. He has become committed to helping his clients think through how they want to live their lives by focusing on "life conversations." Or, in Augie's reference to the 2008 movie with Morgan Freeman and Jack Nicholson, the "bucket list" experience.

Augie's commitment is an excellent example of the notion of "seeking a higher calling" for your work and the role you play in the lives of the people you serve. Recently, a client said that he was bragging about Augie to a friend of his to such a degree that the friend asked for Augie's contact information. The friend then asked Augie's client, "What does he charge?" The answer: "I have no idea, but whatever it is, it's worth it!"

Return to the questions we posed earlier about commitment and give serious thought to what brings purpose and energy to your life and whether you are living life in concert with your priorities and values. If you are not, remember that even small steps can be initiated to bring purpose and accomplishment slowly back to your life.

Perhaps a good place to start would be to contrast the list of words you would hope your clients would use to describe you versus the words you think (or know) they would actually use. Each day look at the two lists and attempt with each client meeting, with each conversation, to move your clients to view you the way you would like to be seen. Each day this activity can bring you to your own "higher calling."

Challenge. The second component of a stress-hardy mindset is *challenge.* Not unexpectedly, stress-hardy people are those who perceive difficult situations as challenges from which to learn rather than opportunities to feel defeated. It is not an easy task when faced with adversity to seek the opportunities that may lie ahead as hidden nuggets in the terrain. But if we fail to undertake the search, we will continue to experience pessimism and stress.

An aspect of challenge is the ability to think outside the box and not be restricted to current ways of perceiving or acting. It involves turning problems into problem solving.

The work of nineteenth-century British physician Dr. Edward Jenner illustrates this feature of stress hardiness. Dr. Jenner strove to find a cure for smallpox, but after studying many cases, he reached an impasse, unable to determine what caused smallpox or what might lead to a cure. However, instead of feeling stuck he shifted his perception of and approach to the problem. What he did may sound quite simple, but in its simplicity was housed its brilliance.

Jenner decided to shift his focus of study from individuals who had contracted smallpox to those who had not. He found that dairymaids rarely were subject to the disease; however, he also discovered that most dairymaids had been afflicted by cowpox, a disease similar to smallpox but one that was usually nonfatal. Jenner hypothesized that the pus in the blisters that dairymaids received from cowpox had served to vaccinate them against the more virile smallpox disease. This led to Jenner's testing his theory by vaccinating individuals with cowpox pus, a procedure that produced a fever but no significant illness. Those injected with the vaccine did not contract smallpox.

The ability to think outside the box, to view finding a cure for a life-threatening disease as a challenge, resulted in Jenner's creation of a vaccine to prevent the contracting of smallpox. He became a pioneer in the field of vaccinations.

In returning to Andrew and Staci, we can see the stress-hardy component of *challenge* in operation. While both faced clients whose well-allocated portfolios had diminished, Staci summoned up the courage to look beyond the current problems to possible opportunities. She met with clients, carefully reviewing their short- and long-term goals and their current portfolio. She did not deny the distress triggered by the significant decrease in the value of the portfolios, but she did not overreact by recommending wholesale changes. She offered recommendations involving some repositioning of particular holdings, sharing thoughts of what she had learned from the economic downturn and the opportunities that existed.

In stark contrast, Andrew could not envision any opportunities that were created in the current economy. While he had appeared confident when the market was rising, he was not prepared for its rapid decline. He was not able to step back and consider new options. Sadly, he became paralyzed. Not knowing what to say or recommend to his clients and feeling like a failure, he retreated from them. Unfortunately, this way of coping was counterproductive and intensified his sense of impotence and incompetence. The negativity of his mindset was hurtling out of control, and all areas of his life were affected.

One might question whether Andrew was capable of adopting Staci's stress-hardy outlook — whether he could think outside the box. We believe that, while the task might seem herculean for Andrew, it is possible. Mindsets and perspectives can be modified, but it becomes more difficult to do so the more our ineffective perceptions and scripts become entrenched. We must keep in mind that we often have more control over what transpires in our lives than we recognize. This brings us to the third "C."

Control (personal). As we emphasized in the last chapter, a basic feature of resilient individuals is that they focus their time and energy on those situations over which they can have some influence, rather than exhausting themselves by attempting to change things over which they have little if any control. The same quality is one of the three features of stress hardiness. A lack of personal control increases the likelihood of emotional and health problems. Unfortunately, as many mental health professionals can verify, countless individuals remain stressed and unhappy because they continue to wait for other people or the situation to change first.

Bob has constantly witnessed this waiting for others to change behavior in his clinical practice. Once, while doing marital therapy, he asked the couple what each thought would enhance their marriage. The wife looked at her husband and responded without a hint that she may have been joking, "I'd be in a good marriage if I weren't married to him." Similar comments involve a parent's saying, "I spank my kids because they make me angry. It's their fault." Or a man telling Bob, "If my boss would only change, I'd be happier."

In what these people are saying there are kernels of truth, but they are hampered by a self-defeating mindset. To achieve personal control we must remember that we are the authors of our own lives — if we aren't happy with a situation, we mustn't blame others or ourselves, but we should ask, "What is it that I can do differently to change the situation?" We will continue to be miserable if we wait for others to make the first move.

Stephen Covey illustrates the importance of personal control in his best-selling book *The Seven Habits of Highly Effective People.* He writes that we all have "circles of concern"; that is, situations or events that bother us. He adds that people who are more effective in life focus on their "circles of influence"; that is, situations or events over which they have some influence.

In his book *A Whack on the Side of the Head,* Roger von Oech offers a powerful illustration of looking within oneself for change rather than assigning responsibility or blame to others. He writes:

> Several years ago I did a seminar with the direct sales force of a large pharmaceutical company. Prior to the session, I had the opportunity to talk to the people in the bottom 25 percent of sales performance. I asked them, "Why aren't you more successful?" They answered with such comments as:
>
> "Our products cost too much."
> "I've got a crummy territory."
> "I don't get along with my manager."
> "The moon is in Sagittarius."

Von Oech then asks, "What was their problem? They weren't taking responsibility for their own performance. They spent their time creating excuses rather than thinking of innovative sales solutions."

He contrasted this more negative, victim-like perspective with the mindset of successful salespeople. He emphasized that the latter group said, "If I get turned down by a physician or nurse, I think of a second way to get business, a third way, and sometimes a fifth way." In essence, the successful group did not wait passively, hoping that factors outside their control would miraculously change. They appreciated that effective change resided within themselves and their proactive behavior.

You might wish to do the following exercise. Write down three things you would like to be different in your life. Next to each indicate whether someone else has to change first for you to achieve your goal. If the goal requires someone else to change first, you would be wise either to cross it off your list or reword it to indicate that you will take the initiative to alter the situation in question.

We can apply the concept of *personal control* to the reactions of Staci and Andrew. Neither had control over the rapid deterioration of the economic situation and market decline. This lack of control or influence is true about many events in our lives, but

Staci and Andrew did have control over their response to this financial downturn.

Staci recognized the personal control she had and took constructive action to deal with the financial crisis. As we noted, she had prepared her clients for a possible downturn, although no one anticipated the depth of the decline. She maintained close contact with her clients and conveyed an air of realistic optimism. Staci's active engagement helped to ease the stress that comes when people feel no control over events in their lives. She actively involved her clients in reviewing different options, which promoted their own sense of control at a time when most felt their financial picture was chaotic.

Very importantly, she recognized that if she became overly stressed her efficacy as an advisor would be appreciably compromised. So she continued to lead a balanced life, addressing her family and personal needs to ensure that her emotional and physical well-being remained intact.

Andrew, as we know, followed a different path, unable to realize the power he had to free himself from negative thoughts and feelings. His professional and personal lives spiraled out of control. A vicious cycle developed in which external economic events hammered the persona he displayed during better times, and he couldn't adapt. Instead of stepping back and considering more constructive options to ease his distress, he became increasingly anxious and depressed. His mentality was that of an angry victim, and as a consequence, he, his family, and his clients suffered.

You are probably wondering whether, given his mindset, Andrew is destined for a life of dissatisfaction and unhappiness. As we emphasized earlier, we believe that need not be the eventual outcome, because mindsets are open to change. For Andrew to accomplish this change, though, he would first have to understand the different components of a stress-hardy mindset and determine whether his feelings, thoughts, and behavior were in accord with these components. If not, he could reflect upon the activities we suggest in this chapter — creating a list of his priorities and values, assessing whether he was leading a life of purpose and balance in accord with these values, identifying what he would like to change in his life, and assessing what changes he had control over.

It requires time and effort to alter our negative mindsets and assume a more stress-hardy professional and personal lifestyle. But as we have seen with Andrew and Staci, the benefits of developing such a mindset and lifestyle far outweigh the struggles we might have in attaining a positive outlook and creating effective coping strategies. Charismatic Advisors are those who strive to understand and adopt a stress-hardy mindset.

Reflections

As an advisor, write down two priorities (purposes) that are most important to you. Reflect upon what you currently do or might do in the future to fulfill these priorities.

List two things you wish could be different as you fulfill your role as an advisor. Ask yourself whether you have control over the factors involved in making these changes and, if so, what steps must you take to realize your goals?

CHAPTER 3

Nurturing Trusting Relationships

Todd Silaika, an extremely accomplished advisor from upstate New York, is meeting with clients Bill Needham and his wife Ann to discuss her portfolio. Bill has been a very substantial client since his retirement seven years before. He also has been a source of some fabulous referrals to others retiring from his department at his former employer. Ann has money from an inheritance four years ago and has been reluctant to consider a serious dialogue with Todd about the portfolio. During the meeting to review Bill's account, Todd had what seemed to be a persuasive rationale for Ann to allow his team to offer some recommendations about her portfolio. She listened, nodded, and smiled but ended the meeting by saying, "Todd, you sure are a good talker."

What was Ann actually saying to Todd? What were the broader implications? Our view is that she was really saying, "Todd, I don't *trust* you." Now, you may counter, "Oh, well, Todd hasn't been able to persuade her to work with him over the past four years so nothing has really changed." That may be, but here's another way to look at it: Perhaps what has changed is her willingness to verbalize her view of Todd, even if not in a totally direct way. A broader implication for Todd is that Ann puts her head down on the pillow next to Bill every night. Might Ann's perception begin to color Bill's perception of Todd, especially when the markets turn ugly?

Todd was actually fortunate, because even though Ann was a bit subtle, it doesn't take a psychologist to figure out what was embedded in her remarks. Often the question of trust is at the forefront of clients' minds, but they may not verbalize it directly. Charismatic Advisors appreciate that *trust* provides the foundation for the work conducted between an advisor and a client, that a relationship not grounded in a deep sense of trust is shaky and insecure at best.

How can an advisor build and reinforce a trusting relationship? Imagine for a moment that you are Todd, having just heard

Ann's comment of being a "good talker." How could you address Ann's perception, to begin to nurture a more trusting relationship? Or would you be reluctant to respond at all, thinking that your understanding of Ann's comments might be off target and bringing it up would actually make it seem that you are trying to read her mind, thereby increasing tension in the relationship? Or if you did misunderstand Ann's comments, could you check it out in a way that would lessen the possible emergence of tension while increasing trust?

These are all important questions that advisors are likely to face at some point in their careers. Later, we will share our thoughts of what Todd might have said or done to develop trust and enhance his relationship with Ann. But first let's examine a little more closely the concept of trust and what it encompasses.

The Experience of Trust

To state the obvious, trust lives at the core of all healthy relationships. A troubled or failed marriage or business alliance can typically be traced to a breakdown in trust. When you need a plumber to fix a clogged drain or are trying to get a haircut while out of town, your mind and gut work in tandem to find the right person to help you. Still, the stakes in these examples aren't very high. If you make a mistake, the worst that happens is that your pipes are still clogged or your hair doesn't become you for several weeks.

When consumers seek advice, however, whether medical, legal, or financial, the stakes are considerably higher and the job of assessing whom to trust can be far more important and complex. Consider for a moment how you process decisions. Suppose you are about to go to the hospital for a procedure. How did you select the hospital? Your approach was probably pretty straightforward — you go where your doctor tells you to go and check in for the procedure. Now think back to just a few years ago, when the media was extensively covering the "widespread" incidence of infections prevalent in hospitals across the country. If it applied to your situation, would this information influence your decisions? Might it even sway you not to check into a hospital at all?

If you extend this analogy to your clients and prospects, it provides some idea of how much skepticism they have about the management of their financial affairs and their decisions associated with financial advice in general. Given everything that has transpired in the recent past, why should investors trust anyone who is in any way, shape, or form associated with Wall Street, a major bank, or the financial services industry in general?

The Elephant in the Room

Clearly, *trust* is a significant elephant in the room. There is more at issue here than just labeling yourself a "trusted advisor." Indeed, the word "trust" isn't brandable. Whom would you trust who says "trust me?" Let's step back and consider the various dimensions of trust.

How might we define what is involved when we use the word "trust?" To assist us in answering that question, think about several people whom you trust, including family or friends and those who serve you in a professional capacity (e.g., your physician, dentist, accountant, electrician, auto mechanic). Jot down the key words you would use to describe them, and then reflect upon specific things they have said or done that prompted you to use these words.

Next, think about several people you don't trust. This lack of trust may have resulted in your ending a relationship or at least minimizing interactions with them. What words would you use to describe these individuals? What specific examples come to mind that contributed to your feeling this lack of trust?

In posing these questions our goal is to encourage you to articulate your criteria for trust and consider ways in which you have used or will begin to use your experiences to guide your behavior with others. As you will discover, your assessment of trust is a complex process, involving both cognitive and emotional dimensions.

David has written of and gives speeches on three dimensions of trust. One dimension is purely **visceral**. You feel it in your gut and in your heart, and it plays a large role in your decision to trust the other person. This is a uniquely individual decision framed by

31

your own experiences and perspectives and is not always easy to articulate. It's a subjective decision, often colored by your sense of whether the person in question genuinely seems interested in your ideas and feelings.

The preliminary litmus test to get a passing grade on the visceral level is a sense of likeability. It's rare for people to begin the process of trust if their initial reaction to someone is dislike or even neutrality. We have all heard the expression, "People do business with people they like." An alternative and perhaps more accurate phrase should be, "People will *not* consider doing business initially with someone they *don't* like." Of course, the same person may be perceived as likeable by one individual but not by another.

So how can you begin to encourage someone to like you in a first meeting or a chance introduction? Think about the last person you met at a party or a meeting whom you liked. Chances are she was a person who asked you questions about yourself and your interests but not in an intrusive or prying way. She seemed genuine about getting to know you without ulterior motives or hidden agendas (e.g., to elicit business from you). Rather than monopolize the conversation by talking about herself or her work, she provided ample opportunities for you to share your "story" with her. Indeed, the more she focused on asking you questions about *you* and genuinely wanted to learn more about you, typically, the more you liked her.

While the first dimension of trust is subjective, a visceral reaction to whether "someone likes you," the second dimension is more **objective.** A client or prospect is wondering, "Do I believe that you are informed, thoughtful, and intelligent in your approach in helping my family achieve our goals?" Simply put: "Do I trust you to dispense sound advice with discipline, objectivity, and perspective?" Even more simply, "Are you actually any good at what you profess you do for a living?" You may have an appealing personality, but if clients question your competency as an advisor, they are unlikely to enter into a relationship with you. This is particularly vital in the aftermath of a difficult period.

In today's complex financial world, there are clear ways to reach this objective standard with prospects and clients. It relates to how seriously you are staying current with what is happening and how crisply you can articulate a thesis or set of theses about what may happen around the corner. Study historic patterns of difficult times, and find the analogies to what's taking shape today. It's not about a dogmatic view but rather an informed opinion, with the humility to fully appreciate that the markets can make you feel and look stupid in the eyes of your clients. It's not about "picking a bottom." It's about your client or prospect's appreciating that you are "in the game" and are continuing to consider what alternative strategies may be in the best financial interest of each client. It's about your client's feeling that you have involved him as an active participant.

Rebecca Rothstein is a very successful advisor based in Beverly Hills. *Barron's* consistently ranks her either #1 or #2 in the top female advisor rankings nationwide. One of Rebecca's unique strengths lies in her ability to generate trust quickly. How? Several team members suggest it rests squarely in her capacity to look at client portfolios during a very first meeting and provide a clear opinion on her view of the potential shortcomings in the client's existing strategy. Rebecca shuns "pitch books" and prefers to operate in real time, getting to the heart of a prospect's issues as she sees it.

A third dimension of trust is **experiential**. What does the actual client experience feel like? It ties directly to being empathic and attempting to see the world through the eyes of your clients, as well as actively reflecting upon your own experiences with other people, some of whom you trust, some of whom you don't. Specifically, do you attempt to understand how your actions are interpreted by the client? Do you try to see the world through their eyes? Do you think about which actions create trust — and which don't? As we noted earlier in this chapter, do you consider actions taken by others that have reinforced or diminished trust in the relationship?

Examining Trust More Closely

While it may appear that the visceral, objective, and experiential foundations of trust differ in how easily each one can be identified, modified, and incorporated into our interactions with clients, this difference may be more illusory than is first apparent. For instance, our intellectual grasp of seemingly objective information may appear straightforward, but consider this: Two advisors may possess comparable financial knowledge but present their information in noticeably different ways to clients, resulting in one's gaining the trust of clients and the other not.

For instance, Larry believes that once he has presented his data, it would be a mistake for a client not to comply with his recommendations. He is quick to minimize or dismiss questions raised by clients, not necessarily in a rude way, but in a manner that suggests, "I am the expert here. Just follow my lead." Larry may not even be aware of how his tone of voice and intense facial expression support his verbal message. Also, he operates on an intellectual plane, frequently missing the emotions that underlie the client's questions. Larry is an expert at designing and discussing charts filled with numbers, but he fails to understand how his focus on data obscures the development of trust.

In contrast, Ian's interactions with clients reflect the mindset of a Charismatic Advisor that was detailed in Chapter 1. Like Larry, he can skillfully describe market variations during the past several decades and explain with clarity issues of allocation and risk. His charts and financial information rival those of Larry, but he understands that without trust even the most carefully prepared data will not be received completely or well by the client. As data are presented, Ian keeps in mind the question rooted in empathic communication; namely, "Am I presenting this data and responding to the client in a way that enriches our relationship?"

Guided by this question, Ian is proactive in his approach to garner trust. Prior to presenting data, he informs his clients that based on the discussion he has had with them, he has prepared information and recommendations for their review. He emphasizes that he welcomes their questions and input, since the final decision about their portfolio falls on their shoulders. He states that if questions remain a decision does not have to be made today, that it is more important to give adequate consideration to all the information presented. He voices genuine appreciation for questions, observing that they help him understand the client's concerns so he is able to respond to these concerns with greater focus.

The objective knowledge possessed by Larry and Ian may be on the same level, but their presentations to clients are likely to evoke different reactions.

Bernie Madoff and the illusions of trust. Trust can be destroyed in a moment — what more powerful, distressing example than that of Bernie Madoff, a man who conducted the largest Ponzi scheme ever witnessed. He attracted a very wealthy clientele and created the image that it was a privilege to allow him to manage their money.

While a few isolated voices warned of his practices and questioned the huge returns he was earning for his clients, especially in a down market, even the SEC did not discover his duplicity. When the Ponzi scheme was revealed, many of his clients were understandably filled with anger and a sense of betrayal, voicing how much they had trusted him. They believed in his brilliance. Most likely, the fact that he managed substantial assets for a number of philanthropic organizations added to his image as a caring, trustworthy person.

Unfortunately, there will always be individuals who recruit psychological principles for their own nefarious purposes in order to get others to do what they want. Their motives are not predicated on benefiting others but rather on filling their own coffers at any cost to those they are supposedly serving. However, while the principles or guidelines of eliciting trust can be misused and abused, thankfully, most advisors will apply these guidelines in a moral and ethical way. We should not allow a handful of uncaring, selfish people to detract from our understanding of the components that contribute to a trusting relationship.

Here are some practical suggestions to nurture trust.

Care first for the client and not the portfolio. Obviously, clients are concerned about the value of their portfolio. They want to see the value of their assets grow as a result of your advice. However, if they are to trust you in both good and bad times, they must feel that you genuinely care about them, that you have expended time and energy to get to know them beyond their finances, and that you understand and are involved in relevant issues surrounding their immediate and extended family. When you learn that your client's favorite nephew just lost his job and is out interviewing, do you simply say, "That's a shame," or do you offer help? "I'm not sure whether I can be of help, but I would be happy to meet with Jimmy to brainstorm career options and perhaps help him with interview skills."

Do you ask them about other specific family members they have mentioned to you before (e.g., an elderly parent or a child who was just admitted to college)? Do you initiate a call when market conditions begin to change to review their allocations? Have you considered the benefits of sending a birthday card with a personal note included? One of our favorite activities is to suggest advisors call clients on their birthdays — but not just to sing a song. Instead, ask a question that positions you as *the* Charismatic Advisor in their lives. "Happy birthday, Joe. You're 64 today; amazing, isn't it? What might be one thing you want to accomplish this year that, left on your own, you might not manage? Would you like me to be the advocate of this goal, to help you make sure it happens before I sing your next birthday wish?"

Every few years, when Bob forgets to bend his knees while lifting something heavy, he visits a chiropractor to help straighten his back. He always sees the same chiropractor because he has great trust in him. Not only has Bob been impressed with the time the chiropractor takes to explain details of his procedure and to answer questions, but he asks about Bob's family and sends a birthday card each year with a note.

Little gestures often go a long way in creating a caring atmosphere.

Be accessible and available. In the field of psychotherapy, a common complaint Bob hears is voiced by people who have had or still have therapists who take several days to respond to phone calls. Some relay the frustration and annoyance they experienced after calling their therapist several times before their call was returned.

At his workshops, especially those for therapists, Bob often asks participants if they have ever waited for hours for a physician or other professional to return a phone call. Almost all answer in the affirmative, and they readily share their frustration at waiting, acknowledging that they know the professional might be having a busy day. However, even if a professional is busy, a brief phone call from him or an assistant to set up a time to talk later in the day (unless it is an emergency situation) is invaluable in creating a caring, trusting relationship.

Recently, David had an episode of brief blurred vision in one eye and called his ophthalmologist, Dr. Don. The doctor returned David's call almost immediately, asked a number of questions, and then concluded that it was probably nothing. He called back again the next morning and said, "I've been thinking about you and would like to review your symptoms with your primary care doctor just to be sure this is not related to something else."

David gave him Dr. Ron's number (believe it or not, the names herein are real!) and, prior to saying goodbye, Dr. Don reassured him that there was probably no reason for concern. Twenty minutes later, Dr. Ron called, asked a number of questions, and then scheduled David for a few tests. He was concerned but not alarmed. Within two days the tests were done, and the results revealed that David was fine.

The recounting of this brief episode should explain why David trusts Drs. Don and Ron. They are accessible, caring, responsive, proactive, and thorough, true professionals in every sense of the word. Consider your own similar personal stories. As suggested earlier, when you think about the professionals whom you rely upon in your life, what are the words you would use to describe them? Why do you trust them? Then ask yourself, "How do I stack up against my own standards of trust?"

Charismatic Advisors step into the trust conversation actively. These advisors tend to have clients describe them in an impassioned way. As asked in Chapter 1, "What are the words you would hope your clients use to describe you to their friends or family?" Would they describe you as "decisive, caring, nurturing, responsive, consistent, current, passionate, genuine, giving, 'in my corner,' straightforward, informed, thoughtful, accessible, sincere,

trustworthy"? These ideas squarely relate to referrals and branding, topics that will be discussed in Chapter 9.

**Practice empathy, empathic communication, and active listen-
ing.** In Chapter 1 and again in this chapter when describing Larry
and Ian, we discussed empathy and empathic communication as
basic skills of a Charismatic Advisor. We would like to expand on
these concepts and highlight an important feature of empathic
communication; namely, *active listening.* By the latter we are refer-
ring to the ability to understand what your client is telling you on
both a cognitive and an emotional level before you respond too
quickly. While expressive language is a major component of
communication, we must begin, as author Stephen Covey reminds
us, by ensuring that we first understand before seeking to be
understood.

Active listening requires you as an advisor to comprehend
both the verbal and nonverbal messages being conveyed by clients; to perceive the feelings, thoughts, and beliefs they are communicating; and to not permit your agenda or preconceived
assumptions about the motives of clients to undermine your ability to appreciate what they are attempting to communicate. We all
have experienced discussions in which we felt the other person
was not really listening to what we had to say; most likely, we
have all engaged in the same behavior at times, jumping in before
understanding the message (certainly, as spouses or parents this
may have occurred more than once, eliciting the response, "You
never listen to me!").

Returning to Todd. At the beginning of the chapter, we described a vignette involving an advisor, Todd. Ann Needham, the
wife of one of his clients who had significant assets apart from her
husband's that were not being handled by Todd but whose business Todd sought, said, "Todd, you sure are a good talker." We
understood her remark as conveying a lack of trust in Todd and
questioning his motives. Although Todd was handling her husband's finances successfully, it appeared that she felt he was trying to manipulate her into doing business with him.

If one listens actively and appreciates the implications of her
statement, it provides an avenue for responding with empathy.
What might Todd have said? Should he have said anything? Not

to respond at all might convey the message that she was correct in her assessment of Todd. However, to respond defensively (e.g., "You don't seem to believe what I say, but look at how much I have helped your husband") is not likely to gain her trust.

We suggest it would be best for Todd to first try to understand and validate what Ann said. Let's see how that might sound.

"Ann, I may be wrong, and please let me know if I am, but when you said that I am a good talker, it seemed as if you were saying I was trying to put one over on you or that I had some ulterior motives in wanting to work with you. If that's so, I'd really like to talk further with you about it, since who would want to work with someone they don't trust? And I certainly would like to work with you."

In this statement Todd is not telling Ann she doesn't trust him (people don't like others to read their minds) but rather raises it as a possibility. He also conveys that he understands that a lack of trust would interfere with their working together, and he states the goal that he would like to work with her.

If Ann responds that her comment about being a good talker was not intended to suggest she didn't trust Todd's motives, he can reply, "I'm glad to hear that — if at any time I say or do something that you question, please let me know." Todd can then recommend a follow-up meeting to suggest ideas for her consideration.

If Ann counters that she does feel that all Todd is after is her business and is not really interested in her, he can reply that he regrets she feels that way, that he certainly wants to work with her, but if he has said or done anything to suggest that he only cares about managing her portfolio and not about her, he would like to know what it is. He can emphasize that gaining her trust is a number one priority for him. Hopefully, this will lead to a follow-up meeting in which the issue of trust can be considered more candidly.

Be open and honest. In addition to seeing adults in his clinical practice, Bob sees children and adolescents and is frequently asked by parents and other caregivers whether and how to discuss difficult topics with youngsters (e.g., the terminal illness of a relative, financial reversals in the household, marital problems).

Bob's advice is that children can sense when something is wrong, and thus to remain silent in hopes of protecting the child is tantamount to saying, "We don't think we can tell you since it would be too upsetting and you won't be able to handle it."

What Bob recommends is to discuss difficult topics honestly with children but to use language that they can understand and to respect issues of privacy (e.g., marital infidelity). The unknown tends to be far more scary and confusing than the known danger. A key issue is that when we inform children of distressing news, we also provide a sense of protection and security. For example, if a parent is diagnosed with a life-threatening disease, a child should be told the parent is ill, but we should add that the doctors are doing everything they can to help and that the other parent or relatives are there to make certain the child is well taken care of. The news will still be distressing, but at least the child can more easily incorporate what is being said since he or she feels protected.

While clients should never be viewed as children needing to be protected from the truth, the parallel to Bob's example is that they want to feel that their advisor is being truthful, open, and honest with them. They want to feel that the advisor will acknowledge if a certain repositioning did not prove financially sound given the downturn (or upturn) in the market. They want to feel that in recommending certain strategies, the advisor is being forthright in reviewing the pros and cons of the proposed strategies. While compliance rules may dictate this openness, clients nevertheless want to believe that their advisors would practice this openness even without the existence of legal regulations.

Be collaborative. As mentioned in Chapter 1, collaboration is a key to working successfully with a client. It is the bridge from a client's getting to know us to her getting to *trust* us. The building of this bridge can be facilitated by directly sharing with the client the view that the relationship is a collaborative one and that if at any time the client is uncertain of what the advisor is saying, she should let the advisor know. A Charismatic Advisor recognizes that any elephants in the room interfering with the advisor-client relationship should be identified, especially when these elephants impede the development and maintenance of trust.

One of the most difficult balancing acts for advisors is the ability to have a clear opinion as to what is in a client's best interest, while also developing and maintaining a collaborative working relationship. If a client feels that a strategy was imposed based only upon the advisor's view, then as soon as markets disappoint, the client will lay the blame at the advisor's doorstep. So the ability to nurture a sense of ownership in clients is a clear priority. Charismatic Advisors are extremely attuned to the importance of this balance. Let's reflect upon some of the insights offered by Augie Cenname, Lori Van Dusen, and John Rafal on this critical topic.

Recall Lori's comment about being "decisive in your opinion, yet collaborative in your approach." She communicates this philosophy both indirectly and directly. Indirectly, whether she is dealing with an investment board at a university or the patriarch or matriarch of an affluent family, she focuses on "drawing people to a cause." In so doing, she is able to translate her messages in ways that make things meaningful to them: "This draws them to you." She is sensitive, yet commanding. Directly, she informs clients, "I can share my expertise, but you are a vital partner." Ultimately, she is willing to be quite decisive: "This is why I think you should do this."

Augie Cenname takes a somewhat different approach by focusing on "accepting people for who they are" versus trying to impose on them what he believes to be the "right" course of action for them. This doesn't mean that he is short on opinion; rather, he is mostly focused through discovery on finding out what is most important to the client and then advocating for that position. This allows him to take a position on issues as an advocate for what are the most important things in the client's lives. Augie's view is that this practice is sorely lacking in our industry. His observation is that too many advisors try to change the client's perception of what they should want or need. Such an approach clearly is not likely to lead to a collaborative environment.

John Rafal also nurtures an extremely collaborative environment by helping them manage life's events. John is especially sensitive to "helping people when they are down." In visits with many of John's clients, it becomes clear that they feel he is "in their corner."

Earlier in this chapter we discuss why we believed Todd needed to confront Ann's comment, "You sure are a good talker." We also suggested language that Todd might consider using in that conversation. When we initially suggested these thoughts to Todd he was reluctant to "open a can of worms" and was thinking he would just let it pass. Upon further reflection, Todd appreciated why he should, instead, "step into the trust conversation." A few weeks passed, and he called Ann to request another meeting. Here is how the dialogue evolved on the phone:

Todd: Good morning, Ann, I hope you and Bill are enjoying this beautiful early spring weather. I know that we were just together a few weeks ago, but I would like to see you again to discuss something rather important with you.

Ann: Todd, you normally deal with Bill; why are you calling me?

Todd: Because the topic I wish to discuss relates to something that you said in our get-together a few weeks ago. You may not recall, but toward the end of our meeting, when I was summarizing my thoughts, you said that I was a "good talker." I keep thinking about that comment and want to meet to discuss it further.

Ann: (Laughter) Oh, Todd, I was just playing with you. I certainly didn't mean anything by it. You know me!

Todd: And I usually get quite a kick out of your sense of humor. But your comment struck me deeply. You may not have meant it that way, but my view of "good talkers" is of people who are trying to sell me something. So it left me with the sense that you might have felt that I was trying to sell you something. I have known you and Bill for a very long time and have tried to bring as much objectivity and perspective as possible to your financial affairs. I never think of my role as being here to sell you anything. My role is to help you identify and reach your life goals through retirement with as few worries as possible.

Ann: I know you always have our interests at heart, and I am sorry that you took my comment so seriously. It was not intended to be hurtful. There is absolutely no need for you to drive down here to meet with us. As my grandchildren say, "We're all good."

The conversation moved on from there, and ultimately, Ann did entrust Todd with some of her personal assets. More importantly, Todd had reinforced how he wanted Ann and Bill to view him. Instead of avoiding the elephant in the room, he called it out directly.

Reflections

Think about three difficult conversations you have had with different clients. What made those discussions difficult? Do you think the clients were expressing a diminished sense of trust in you? Were you pleased with how you responded in each situation? If not, why not? How might you respond differently today? If you were pleased with how you responded in one situation, but not the others, what did you learn from the situation that you felt you handled more effectively in terms of developing trust?

CHAPTER 4

Having the Insight and Courage to Change Negative Scripts

In Chapter 2 we met two advisors, Andrew and Staci, and examined the strikingly different ways in which they responded to a downturn in the market and in the portfolios of their clients. While Staci adopted a proactive approach, remaining in close contact with her clients and focusing on the factors over which she had some control or influence, Andrew was paralyzed, not knowing what to say or do with clients. He became anxious and depressed and assumed the position of a victim, losing sight of what actions he might initiate to address the difficult financial climate.

Andrew's negative mindset, including his lack of confidence, found expression in behaviors that we call negative scripts; that is, his self-defeating thoughts resulted in anxiety and the repeated use of counterproductive coping strategies. In contrast, Staci's more optimistic outlook guided her to design scripts to successfully manage challenging events rather than being defeated by them.

We Are the Authors of Our Own Lives

We all follow scripts in life, certain patterns of predictable behaviors. Scripts, if not rigidly applied, help to bring order and consistency to one's life. If these patterns result in satisfaction, if they nurture positive relationships, and if they allow flexibility and change, they deserve to be repeated. However, when our words and actions, constantly repeated, are self-defeating or ineffective, it is prudent to modify or abandon them. Yet many individuals, similarly to Andrew, continue to follow these negative scripts, sometimes even more forcefully with each passing day, believing that at some point the negative script will lead to positive results.

If we are dissatisfied with certain features of our lives or if we find ourselves persistently engaging in thoughts or behaviors that lead to frustration, anger, and unhappiness, then it is our responsibility to take the initiative to rewrite the negative scripts that are causing us such distress. We must remember that **we are the authors of our own lives**. As authors we have more control than we may realize to alter many parts of the script that result in unhappiness. We need not be trapped by behaviors that have proven ineffective.

Although it is easy to utter or write the words, "We are the authors of our own lives," for many it is a herculean task to assume this role. Instead, we continue to adhere to behaviors that are unproductive, seemingly not learning from past mistakes. You may ask this reasonable question: "Why do many people experience noticeable difficulty in recognizing, acknowledging, and then changing their course of action when this action proves counterproductive?"

Therapists like Bob have witnessed numerous examples of patients who repeat actions that cause them much grief. Unfortunately, some predictable, self-defeating patterns of behavior become increasingly entrenched. These negative scripts serve to constrict people and weaken their ability to assume personal control or responsibility for their lives. We may not even be aware that we are following negative scripts because they have become a "natural part" of our existence. Even if we recognize the existence of these scripts, we may feel powerless to change them, similar to what Andrew experienced, especially as he became overwhelmed by anxiety. Some individuals maintain negative scripts as they persistently wait for other people or situations to change to meet their needs. As mentioned earlier, Bob has frequently heard people say that the only thing keeping them from feeling happy is that someone else continues to engage in behaviors that annoy them.

An illustration of the sense of helplessness that can pervade a person's life and reinforce the repetition of self-defeating attitudes and behavior is seen in Lou, a man in his 30s who came to see Bob for therapy. Lou complained of having been "scatterbrained and disorganized since childhood." He said that he frequently forgot where he placed things such as his keys; he neglected to follow through on certain responsibilities at work (he was fired from one job); and he had an inordinate amount of difficulty getting ready in the morning, frantically searching for his clean clothes or papers he needed for work. He told Bob, "I have been diagnosed with ADHD [attention deficit hyperactivity disorder], so that's why I have trouble organizing my life. I've tried medication, but that doesn't seem to help, and I've also had some side effects from the medication. I guess I'll just have to live this way."

Lou accepted as a given that his diagnosis of ADHD meant that he was incapable of modifying those behaviors that produced significant stress in his life. He felt bound by a negative script that did not invite modification. Since Lou did not entertain the possibility of change, Bob asked what prompted him to seek therapy. Rather than take responsibility for calling Bob for an initial appointment, Lou simply said, "My internist thought it would be a good idea since I'm feeling so anxious and depressed, and I've also had stomachaches and headaches."

Bob wondered, "That's how your internist sees things. What do you think?"

Lou responded, "Quite honestly, I called because my internist recommended that I do so, but without wishing to sound disrespectful, I don't think therapy can change my ADHD."

Bob answered, "I'm glad you're being so honest about what you're thinking. I have some sense of how you're feeling. I agree that therapy can't change the fact that you have ADHD. However, what I think we can accomplish working together is to find more effective ways for you to deal with the struggles you're having related to ADHD."

The intent of this last comment was to validate Lou's perception that he couldn't change the fact he was born with ADHD but that he could learn more adaptive strategies for coping with the behaviors associated with ADHD. Bob was attempting to introduce the notion that particular negative scripts, while practiced for years, were open to change. In fact, much of the therapeutic work with Lou involved implementing techniques for dealing with his disorganization. These included keeping a small basket on a shelf by the door to place his keys, selecting and laying out his clothes in the evening so the morning was less hectic, and doing the same for the documents he had to bring to work.

While these strategies might seem very obvious, they were not to Lou, given his mindset that his behaviors were rooted in a disorder that did not allow for change.

Financial Advisors and the Presence of Negative Scripts

As David travels the country coaching financial advisors against the backdrop of very challenging capital markets, he hears negative scripts virtually every day. A classic example is, "I hear about all of the 'money in motion,' yet somehow I don't have the time to reach out to new prospective clients. I am spending *all* of my time just trying to hold on to the clients I already have!"

Doesn't this sound a bit like Lou? The question David usually poses when he hears this remark is, "Really? How much time are you actually spending helping your clients cope with the problems caused by severe net worth diminution?" Upon serious reflection, advisors begin to recognize that this is a negative script and that they are using this as a rationalization to avoid the difficult challenges of identifying and cultivating new clients. One can easily fall into the trap of avoiding what seems to be a challenging task even when this way of coping is self-defeating.

Questions that advisors can ask themselves to assess whether they are engaged in a negative script such as the one described above might be the following:

- How am I *really* spending my time?
- Am I spending significant time on things I can control or things over which I have no control?
- Do I spend much of my day being reactive?
- Am I spending more time with e-mails than in conversations?
- Am I *really* spending so much time nurturing existing clients, or am I spending time *thinking* about the need to nurture clients?

"The Busy Trap"

David has written about and speaks regularly with advisors on what he calls "The Busy Trap." This concept is an example of "predictable, self-defeating patterns of behavior" caused by negative scripts. The busy trap manifests itself in wasted time and disorganized days. For some advisors it's a fixation on the moment-by-moment moves of volatile markets. For others it's the time spent on reading and responding to e-mails. As David often points out, "Back in the old days we had a little rectangular object on the corner of our desks. What was it? That's right, it was called an 'in box,' and the mail came once or maybe twice a day. You looked at it when you were good and ready to. Now, advisors are getting bombarded by e-mails literally every minute, and many feel the compulsion to look at them as soon as they hit the screen. How can one possibly keep to a rhythm in a day with that kind of ongoing distraction?"

Some good old-fashioned time blocking could do wonders to free advisors up for more proactive activities.

Advisors have to be aware of and then modify their own negative scripts if they are to assume the role of a Charismatic Advisor. Once advisors have grappled with their own busy traps, they can then confront the difficult, yet vital, task of helping clients address their unique negative scripts.

A Warning: Don't Attempt to Change Negative Scripts Too Rapidly

At this point we want to identify a situation that may occur when people attempt to modify negative scripts that have burdened their lives. Bob has found in his clinical practice that one of the best predictors that new scripts will fail is when people introduce these new patterns of behavior without careful consideration of how realistically achievable they are. While we are strong advocates of changing those scripts that are counterproductive, we also caution about implementing new scripts that are destined to fail.

Bob recalls Glenn Dalton, who came to see him because of work-related stress. Glenn was spending more than 60 hours a week at work. When Bob asked him to identify his priorities in life, Glenn listed his roles as a husband and father as singularly important to him. Yet, in reality, he was so consumed with his work that he spent little time with his wife or his children. He frequently did not get home from work until 9:00 or 9:30 in the evening, long after his two young children were asleep. In recognizing the need to adopt a new script, Glenn asserted, "Starting next week I am going to be home in time for dinner every night."

Glenn was somewhat surprised when Bob cautioned, "Don't even try to do that."

"Why not?"

Bob responded, "I think it's great that you want to make changes, but I've found that when people try to change things too quickly, when the changes are not realistic and open to failure, they often become angry with themselves or others and revert to their old behaviors."

Glenn interrupted, "But I think I can be home for dinner on time."

"I know you would like to do so, and I think that's great, but you're so accustomed to getting home at 9:00 or later, I wonder how realistic it will be for you to get home at 6:00 each night. I think that while a long-range goal might be to be home each night for dinner, it might make more sense to start by getting home early on one night and building from there."

Bob continued, "When we make changes, we should program ourselves for success. For example, too many people begin diets or exercise in a frantic way and then feel worse when they can't maintain the pace they have started."

Glenn said he understood Bob's point. He followed Bob's recommendation, establishing as a goal coming home for dinner on Friday evenings, which was the evening he felt would be easiest to leave the office on time. Eventually, he expanded his family dinners to three evenings a week, which, on a regular basis, turned out to be achievable.

Client Negative Scripts Brought on by Difficult Market Conditions

Bob's intervention with Glenn has relevance for financial advisors. For example, advisors must suggest realistic goals to those clients who become panicky when their portfolios begin to fall, then impulsively desire to replace or abandon their existing script (portfolio, financial plan) by selling all their equities and having their assets strictly in cash. A portfolio that has been carefully planned should be open to modification when the financial environment changes, but this does not imply the need for a drastic change borne out of anxiety.

Todd Silaika, the advisor we met in the last chapter, understood the importance of adapting sensibly to external stresses rather than resorting to changes that were emotionally based, changes that for all intents and purposes threw out financial plans that had been thoughtfully developed and implemented. Here is one example of an e-mail Todd sent to his clients:

In 2003 I was at Disney World with my family. My oldest two daughters, Karen and Vicky, both wanted to go on Space Mountain, the roller coaster at Magic Kingdom. The three of us decided it would be fun to go on the ride. It had been 25 years since I was on that roller coaster. I tried to recall my memory to Vicky of how scary this ride would be but clearly misstated the facts. We started out waiting in line, which looked reasonably short but was extremely long. Vicky fell asleep, and I carried her all the way up the line in my arms. By the time we got to the top, an hour had passed, and we were committed. My oldest, Karen, was tired but excited, and I was just tired. Now we were ready to begin the ride. At this point Vicky became very nervous. She began protesting the ride, looking for a way out. I calmed her nerves and explained that we had come this far and could not turn back at this point. She finally agreed to continue.

We entered the roller coaster seats, and instantly, there was more protest. If you have ever been on Space Mountain, you may remember you do not sit next to anyone, but rather in a row. So you sit alone. We were buckled in and started on our path. I told Vicky that it was not that scary, and I would be with her the entire time. I told her the ride did not go upside down as well. Clearly, I was wrong. As the ride progressed faster and faster, I could hear the tears flowing from the seat in front of me. Then everything went pitch black. We raced along the track, hurtling through "space," and Vicky was crying every step of the way. As the roller coaster looped upside down and I heard her yell, a tremendous feeling of guilt came over me. I felt horrible. The three-minute ride felt like an eternity. The tears stopped once we left the ride, but when Vicky saw my wife, she began crying all over again. This time she was not alone. Before long I was in tears, along with Beth and the kids! The outcome of this trip was not the expectation I had of a day at Disney's Magic Kingdom.

You are probably wondering what in the world this has to do with stocks or bonds. This morning our team had our normal Monday briefing. As you can all imagine, the tone was hardly sanguine. As we discussed the current environment, my partner, Scott, was comparing the market to a roller coaster ride. That was when I remembered this story from my past. My team here feels the same emotions today that I felt when my daughter was on Space Mountain. The most bearish economists 15 months ago were suggesting that the Dow could fall to 10,500 from 14,000 – a true bear market drop of 25 percent. Today the Dow closed at 6,763. Now suggestions are that the Dow could fall below 5,000. Was anyone predicting a Dow below 7,000 15 months ago? If so, it would have never made the news.

My biggest fear for investors today is *not* the obvious: that all markets (stock, real estate, commodity, and fixed income) will continue to fall in the short term. My biggest fear is *the less obvious*: that investors go to cash, collect less than 1 percent on their money and either never have enough to retire or end up running out of assets in retirement. This market has unleashed an emotion in almost everyone that is similar to the "fight or flight" reaction we have when facing danger. Emotions drive investors to hold cash with almost no interest or to own a CD at 2 percent, when they could own a short-term government bond that yields 3 percent or a medium-term government bond paying 5 percent.

Warren Buffett published his widely anticipated annual report over the weekend. Here is a piece from the report:

"Whatever the downsides may be, strong and immediate action by government was essential last year if the financial system was to avoid a total breakdown. Had one occurred, the consequences for every area of our economy would have been cataclysmic. Like it or not, the inhabitants of Wall Street, Main Street and the various Side Streets of America were all in the same boat.

"Amid this bad news, however, never forget that our country has faced far worse travails in the past. In the 20th century alone, we dealt with two great wars (one of which we initially appeared to be losing), a dozen or so panics and recessions, virulent inflation that led to a 21½% prime rate in 1980, and the Great Depression of the 1930s, when unemployment ranged between 15% and 25% for many years. America has had no shortage of challenges.

"Without fail, however, we've overcome them. In the face of those obstacles — and many others — the real standard of living for Americans improved nearly *seven*fold during the 1900s, while the Dow Jones Industrials rose from 66 to 11,497. Compare the record of this period with the dozens of centuries during which humans secured only tiny gains, if any, in how they lived. Though the path has not been smooth, our economic system has worked extraordinarily well over time. It has unleashed human potential as no other system has, and it will continue to do so. America's best days lie ahead."

Todd finishes his e-mail by saying,

I agree with Buffett. Please call me to discuss your portfolio if you are losing sleep. Let me spend the time reviewing what you own and why, so we can proceed with caution and care and remain focused on the long-term objective, not just the short-term issues at hand. I do not have enough room in this communication to recite the volumes of bad news we read and see every day. If you want to see the bad news, it is everywhere. The good news is that the Space Mountain ride did end, and we all survived. The good news is that every bear market in history has ended in a bull market. The good news is that this is not the Great Depression.

Todd's letter reflects key features of a Charismatic Advisor, including those that we will highlight in the next chapter; namely, empathy and empathic communication. He displays empathy by sharing a personal experience and conveying an appreciation for the anxieties his clients are experiencing. Once he expresses this understanding, he skillfully discusses the importance of maintaining a sensible course of action and not acting impulsively. His empathy permits his clients to be more receptive to his message of patience. They feel that he truly understands what they are experiencing.

Maintaining Positive Scripts When These Scripts Are Challenged

Todd's actions bring up an important point. Scripts that have led to positive results in the past need not be abandoned when financial outcomes begin to falter. For example, Todd understood that the rapid deterioration in market conditions naturally triggered increased anxiety in his clients. He also recognized that, while some modifications in the portfolios of a number of his clients were necessary, this was not the time to precipitously change his approach to financial advising. Rather, he understood that modifications should fall within the parameters of the path he was on with his clients prior to the current economic downturn. Very importantly, he knew that it was his responsibility to be proactive in communicating his perspective.

Todd reviewed each client's portfolio. While he had always maintained close contact with his clients, he knew that to lessen their panic it was essential that he initiate more contact with them. He especially did so via his thoughtful e-mails, acknowledging the anxiety that everyone was experiencing. He emphasized that he would meet with each of them to discuss possible alterations in their portfolio and that the best course of action was not to take drastic steps. In essence, Todd's adherence to a positive script enabled his clients to remain calm and not resort to adopting a new plan that, while offering temporary relief, might result in the emergence of a new script that was reactive and negative.

Not all advisors follow the steady path demonstrated by Todd and Staci. Certainly, Andrew did not. Nor did Carla, a financial advisor who was very shaken by the turmoil in the financial markets. Similar to the actions of her colleagues, she had always advocated diversification, recognizing that this strategy would differ from one client to the next, depending on such factors as age, years until retirement, and size of portfolio. Her clients respected her thoroughness in reviewing their portfolios and her ability to explain without jargon the language of investments.

Yet, Carla's prudent investment approach, as evidenced by her focus on diverse, seemingly safe stocks and mutual funds, was hit hard by the economic crisis. The portfolios of her clients, which had shown steady growth in recent years, had diminished by 30 to 40 percent over the previous 12 months. Carla lamented, "All of my training and experience didn't prepare me for what has happened this past year. I thought I had a safe investment approach. Now I feel personally responsible for having lost a sizable portion of my clients' assets that they may never recover."

Carla offered an interesting image to describe her current mental state. "In past years I felt as if I was rowing a boat in relatively calm waters and knew exactly where I was heading. Now I feel like I'm in the same boat, but the oars are gone; I'm in very choppy waters, being carried along without any control of where I'm heading."

If we view the steps involved in developing and maintaining an investment plan as a script to follow, it is obvious that Carla's script for years was productive, resulting in financial gains for her clients. Certainly, the healthy financial climate that existed at the time contributed to the positive nature of her approach. However, this seemingly positive script was illusory in the sense that it did not contain flexibility conducive to adapting to the rapidly deteriorating financial picture.

Thus, rather than adhering to a flexible script that would allow her to navigate the current economic crisis with her clients, Carla became more anxious and handled her distress by lessening contact with them. She began to doubt herself. Unlike the calm, practical demeanor demonstrated by Todd, she became caught up in the fears of her clients, and those clients sensed her uncertainty. Unfortunately, they began to lose trust in her.

Changing Less Obvious Negative Scripts of Clients

Negative scripts are everywhere in times of severe market volatility, as "woulda, shoulda, coulda" runs rampant. Yet there are many more subtle examples of negative scripts that your clients and prospects can be burdened with for life. Imagine the implications for advisors who are capable of diagnosing such scripts and then being able to help clients shed them. This may be one of the ultimate higher callings of the Charismatic Advisor.

Here are a few examples of such negative scripts that most likely are recognizable to most advisors:

1. Mary is a 71-year-old widow. Her husband Harry died five years ago and left Mary a sizable equity portfolio; she has been living off the dividends. The income is no longer adequate to support her lifestyle, yet she refuses to change her portfolio since "Harry told me to never touch the stocks."

2. Susan is married to William. William makes a very good, but not a spectacular, income. No matter how much Susan and William seem to accumulate in the way of assets, Susan always feels poor. She constantly reminds William of what she perceives to be their precarious financial existence. Her financial insecurity impacts William's sense of personal success, which reinforces his own feelings of failure, often paralyzing him from taking realistic risks. A vicious cycle operates to maintain a negative script.

3. Jill and Jack have been married for 30 years and rarely agree about how to invest their money. Jill explains: "Whatever decisions we make with our money are *always* wrong. Actually, they are more Jack's decisions than mine, since he feels that I don't know much about finances. He gives me no credit for having some intelligence." They consult with an advisor, and Jill says, "I hope you'll listen to me."

4. Joseph is a 62-year-old physician. He feels burned out and would like to retire as soon as possible. His wife, Samantha, explains: "He can't retire; he has no hobbies — he won't know what to do with himself." Their financial advisor senses that the roots of Samantha's comments are housed in anxieties about their net worth and whether, given their lifestyle, they can really afford to have Joseph retire.

A key component of Bob's therapeutic work is to help patients become more aware of the ineffective scripts in their lives and then work with them to change these scripts. Financial advisors often face the same task that Bob does; namely, to change the scripts of clients that compromise their financial situations. However, some client scripts are not easily dislodged and are rooted in strong emotions.

Reflections

The four scenarios above illustrate the challenges advisors face. Think for a moment about each of these examples. Then ask yourself, "What would I say or do to help alter these seemingly negative scripts?" For example, consider Mary, and ask yourself: "If Mary were my client, how would I approach her, what would I say and do so that she will be receptive to altering her current view, a view that may be difficult to change since it represents her husband's dying wishes?" In the next chapter about empathy and empathic communication, we will offer some suggestions for working with clients like those described in our four vignettes who may be stuck in a particular script.

CHAPTER 5

Empathy and Empathic Communication

In Chapter 1 we introduced the concept of empathy as an integral quality of a Charismatic Advisor. As we noted, empathy is the ability to place oneself in the shoes of another person and to see the world through their eyes. Empathy is sometimes confused with sympathy, but they are quite different. Sympathy involves feeling sorry for someone, while empathy is associated with appreciating the other person's perspective.

In Chapters 2 and 3 we offered examples of advisors who displayed empathy, such as Todd, Staci, and Ian, and those who for certain reasons did not, such as Andrew and Larry. We ended the last chapter with four case vignettes and asked how an advisor might respond effectively to each of the clients portrayed. Before we return to these vignettes and offer examples of dialogue that a Charismatic Advisor might use, it will be helpful to define the concepts of empathy and empathic communication and examine their significance in day-to-day interaction.

Defining Empathy

Empathy significantly influences the quality of our personal and professional lives, especially those aspects related to social relationships. Empathy enhances communication, cooperation, respect, and compassion. It helps us in modifying negative scripts as we try to enrich our interactions with others. As noted earlier, Daniel Goleman described empathy as an essential feature of emotional intelligence (EQ) and in his later work afforded it a major role in social intelligence. In his book *Primal Leadership: Realizing the Power of Emotional Intelligence*, Goleman and coauthors Richard Boyatzis and Annie McKee reflect upon the role of empathy. They write:

"Empathy is the fundamental competence of social awareness. . . . Empathy is the sine qua non of all social effectiveness in working life. Empathic people are superb at recognizing and

59

meeting the needs of clients, customers, or subordinates. They seem approachable, wanting to hear what people have to say. They listen carefully, picking up what people are truly concerned about, and they respond on the mark."

In Chapter 1 we listed questions that we suggest advisors ask themselves on a regular basis to keep empathy in the forefront of their thinking. To review, the questions included:

- What words would I hope my clients use to describe me?
- What have I said or done in the past few months to make it likely that they would use these words?
- What words would they actually use?
- How do I know what words they would actually use?
- What must I do so that the words they actually use are the same words I *hope* they use?

To answer the question "What words would they actually use?" advisors must consider the ways in which they encourage and obtain feedback from their clients, a process that is best initiated during the first couple of meetings with a prospective client. Advisors can point out that they will be more effective if they seek regular feedback from the clients. We will discuss the issue of feedback in greater detail in Chapter 7 when we highlight the themes of coping strategies and collaboration.

Not only is it important to elicit feedback from new clients, it's also vital to obtain ongoing feedback from longtime clients. If you have not actively solicited constructive criticism from clients, it's never too late to start. Particularly during or in the aftermath of difficult market environments, it is vital to solicit assessments from your clients. Here are questions for you to consider incorporating into year-end reviews in such difficult times:

1. What words come to mind when you think of me and my team and how we have responded to your family during the past year?
2. Do you feel we were successful in reasonably assessing your tolerance for risk before this downturn?
3. Have recent events changed your perspective, plans, dreams, fears? Have those same events created any additional financial pressures (related to, for example, parents, adult children, extended family, employment)?

4. Have you felt that our team has maintained perspective and helped you do the same?
5. Do you feel we have been there for you emotionally? Please elaborate.
6. Are there any particular teammates of mine who you feel could do a better job? Could I? If so, who and how?
7. Do you feel confident that together we will get through this difficult period?
8. If there were one or two things I could do more effectively for you and your family, what might they be?

Positive economic times should not lead to complacency. Soliciting feedback should be an ongoing priority; at the very least it should be integrated into year-end client reviews. The questions you ask should be customized in light of the time in which they are asked and the situation that exists for each specific client.

Empathic Communication

The task of considering how advisors would like to be described by their clients and the ways in which clients would actually describe them is likely to prompt other questions related to the concept of empathic communication. In *The Power of Resilience* Bob and his colleague, Sam Goldstein, pose the following questions:
  *   In anything I say or do, what do I hope to accomplish?
  *   Would I want anyone to say or do to me what I have just said or done with this other person?
  *   Am I saying or doing things in a manner in which other people will be most responsive to listening to what I have to say?
  *   Even if I disagree with others, do I at least validate their point of view, recognizing that validation does not imply I agree with their position but that I at least acknowledge it?
  *   Do I attempt to understand before being understood?

      This is an important question posed by Stephen Covey in his book *The Seven Habits of Highly Effective People* — emphasizing the importance of not rushing into a conversation before reflecting upon what the other person is trying to communicate.

- Do I encourage expressions of feelings and thoughts from others, or do I say and do things that discourage or avoid honest communication, especially about difficult topics?
- Do I model effective communication by listening to what others have to say?

You may find it easier to answer these if you consider the following two questions:

- What makes it easiest for me to listen to what others have to say?
- What do others say or do that turns me off and keeps me from listening to their message?

Bob recalls when he was training director in the psychology department at a psychiatric hospital: Louise, a trainee, voiced being upset with Joan, one of her supervisors. She said that when Joan disagreed with what Louise said to particular patients, she would ask, "Why would anyone say something like that?" Not surprisingly, Louise experienced Joan's feedback as harsh and demeaning.

Louise's remarks triggered memories in Bob of his own days as a trainee and how vulnerable he could feel as he was learning to conduct psychotherapy. He recalled supervisors who, even when questioning Bob's approach, displayed the ability to offer alternative ways Bob might speak with patients while being supportive of his efforts. He also thought of one particular supervisor whom he perceived as consistently critical and from whom it was more difficult to learn.

Bob asked Louise if she had spoken with Joan about her feelings. Louise said she had attempted to, but Joan appeared to dismiss her remarks, contending that Louise had to learn to accept feedback about her performance as a therapist.

In preparing to speak with Joan, Bob was guided by the questions raised earlier about empathic communication. He considered his goal for the meeting; namely, that Joan needed to become aware of her supervisory style to become a more effective, positive teacher. Bob also reflected on how to provide feedback to Joan in a way that would lessen defensiveness and create a collaborative atmosphere. In essence, Bob wanted to model a style of communication that he wished to see adopted by Joan.

Bob began the meeting by discussing positive comments provided by different trainees about Joan's supervisory style. He also emphasized that if Joan was not in agreement with any of his feedback, she should let him know. A comment such as this conveys to the other person that it is okay to hold different perceptions, a message that frequently helps to defuse what could be a tense meeting.

Joan acknowledged that at times she had said to trainees, "Why would anyone say something like that?" noting that it is her way of challenging them to consider more effective ways of communicating with patients.

Bob agreed that it was helpful for trainees to be challenged to think about the words they used with patients. However, he asked Joan to consider if the feedback she was providing might be interpreted as harsh and judgmental, triggering emotions that would work against her goal of having trainees learn from her.

Some readers may be surprised by Joan's initial response, especially since she held a doctorate in clinical psychology, a profession that emphasizes communication skills. She said, "My intention was not to be judgmental, and I'm surprised Louise experienced it that way. I wonder if she is an overly sensitive person." Joan's response placed full responsibility (perhaps blame) on Louise. It is little wonder that Louise felt Joan was dismissive of her feedback.

If you were Bob, consider how you might respond to Joan to maximize the possibility that she would listen and use the feedback she had just received. Bob first validated Joan's observation (remember that validation does not imply agreement), hoping that it would assist her to be more responsive to accepting Louise's evaluation.

Bob said, "It may be that Louise is more sensitive than other trainees, but if that's the situation, then as supervisors we have to offer feedback in ways that she can learn from us. If she feels more comfortable with our feedback, it may even help her to become less sensitive."

Joan listened closely. Bob continued, "What I have found helpful in my supervisory activities is to think about supervisors I had as a trainee — from whom did I learn best and what was their style? I never wanted to be a clone of one of my supervisors, since we all have different styles, but I thought I could 'borrow' from things they said that I found helpful."

This initial dialogue permitted Joan to reflect upon her comments to Louise. In a subsequent meeting with Bob, she was more open to considering how her remarks could be seen as judgmental. She and Bob talked about how, when she disagreed with Louise's response to a patient, she might say, "What you told the patient is one possible response, but if we keep in mind what you hope to accomplish in therapy with this patient, there are other comments you might offer." This last statement represents empathic communication with a heavy dose of validation.

After a couple of meetings with Bob, Joan displayed the courage to offer an important message. "Even though I'm trained as a clinical psychologist, it's important to be reminded of the different ways we might say things that help people learn from us rather than make them more defensive."

As an advisor think of situations you experienced with clients that did not go as smoothly as you would have wished. To assume the role of a Charismatic Advisor, ask, "What is it that I could have said or done differently that might have improved this meeting?"

Obstacles to Empathy and Empathic Communication

Bob was once asked at a workshop, "If empathy is such an important attribute, why is it so difficult to be empathic?" If we are to be Charismatic Advisors, an answer to this question is essential. Let's review four notable factors that lessen empathy.

1. It is far easier to be empathic toward those people who agree with our ideas or respond according to the ways we desire. As an advisor you should think about those clients who are more cooperative and who rarely, if ever, display sarcasm or anger. It's less challenging to understand their point of view because they tend to be more open to listening to us with an unbiased mind. We enjoy meeting with them. In contrast, empathy may suffer when we meet a client such as Art Lansing (see Chapter 1), who quickly questions why he needs to see an advisor and wonders what the advisor's track record is. As we noted, an insecure advisor, when confronted with a client such as Art, might be thrown by his forceful, challenging nature, minimizing the advisor's attempt to understand Art's perspective and work with it.

In his workshops for parents, Bob tells them, "It's easier to be empathic toward our children when they listen to what we say and are cooperative." He jokingly adds, "And it's easier to be empathic when our kids wake up each morning and say, 'I am so fortunate to be a member of this household.' Of course, if they say that, it may be cause for suspicion."

A formidable challenge for an advisor is to be empathic when you are interacting with people with whom you are annoyed, frustrated, or even angry. When such emotions are present, one must step back and think about what is triggering your negative emotions. You should also consider the questions posed earlier in this chapter, including these: "What do I hope to accomplish?" and "Am I saying or doing things in a manner in which other people will be most responsive to listening to what I have to say?"

2. Whether we realize it or not, we are constantly making assumptions about why others act the way they do. Our perception of the motives of others, which is rooted in our mindset, influences our response to their actions. Far too often we neglect to realize that these are *our* assumptions and that equally plausible alternative assumptions may exist. Empathy is weakened when we make assumptions about the motives of others that may, in fact, not be accurate, but we respond as if they represent the *truth*.

To use Art Lansing once more as an illustration, a Charismatic Advisor might welcome Art's challenging behavior and not interpret it as hostile. As we showed in Chapter 1, such an advisor, free of anxiety or self-doubt, will be better equipped to understand Art's perspective and say, "Art asks challenging questions, but I'm glad he does. I'd rather have his concerns right out in the open so I can address them, rather than have them hidden." A less secure advisor might quickly label Art as an angry, belligerent person and interpret his motives in a very negative manner, keeping the advisor from attempting to understand what is prompting Art's questions.

We're not saying that our understanding of the motives of others is inaccurate but that it is best to recognize and consider other viewpoints of why people act the way they do or, as we will discuss in the next chapter, why they are using certain coping strategies. More constructive interactions can result from our efforts to be more understanding.

As Marilee Adams eloquently explains in her book *Change Your Questions, Change Your Life*, we always have the fundamental choice of going down either the path of the "learner" or the path of the "judger." The learner path is the path of discovery and allows us to focus on asking, "What are they thinking, feeling, and wanting?" which in turn leads us to "seeing with new eyes, hearing with new ears." This mindset keeps us from too quickly making assumptions and instead leads to the role of "nonjudgmental observer." This kind of openness lies at the core of one's ability to be truly empathic.

3. A third common obstacle to empathy is the misperception that if you're too empathic people will take advantage of you. Bob often hears this complaint in his clinical work and seminars. In *The Power of Resilience*, an illustration is offered of a businessman who voiced concern that if he were too empathic his business would suffer, explaining, "If I stop to think about how I come across to my employees and how they would describe me, I think it would keep me from acting decisively. I would second-guess every decision I made, wondering how they felt about it. They aren't motivated to do what I tell them to do now. Imagine what would happen if I were less decisive."

At Bob's parenting seminars, these sentiments are voiced repeatedly by mothers and fathers who fear that empathy will compromise their ability to set limits and apply consequences, leading them to raise spoiled children.

It's unfortunate that many individuals confuse empathy and empathic communication with not being decisive or honest, of becoming a doormat on which others could trample. If anything, we believe that empathy provides the fuel for increased decisiveness and honesty. Empathic people don't refrain from giving others feedback or setting appropriate limits; instead, they do so in a way that makes it likely that these others will listen and respond positively to what they have to say, as Bob discovered in his dialogue with Joan.

Empathic people don't compromise their values or allow themselves to be belittled but rather express their viewpoint in ways that will lessen defensiveness. If people feel taken advantage of, it's most likely a result of their not knowing how to set realistic limits or worrying that others will be angry with them. Goleman, Boyatzis, and McKee capture this position when they write:

"But empathy . . . doesn't mean a kind of 'I'm okay, you're okay' mushiness. It doesn't mean that leaders would adopt other people's emotions as their own and try to please everybody. That would be a nightmare — it would make action impossible. Rather, empathy means taking employees' feelings into thoughtful consideration and then making intelligent decisions that work these feelings into the response."

4. A fourth obstacle involves what we call "self-orientation." It's difficult to be empathic if we're too focused on ourselves. Prospects and clients can often feel this, and it not only can erode likability but also can dramatically diminish a feeling of trustworthiness. In speeches to financial advisors across the country, David often talks about the "big dog effect." The advisor and prospect start talking, and the advisor poses questions, but somewhere along the line he feels the need to insert his ego. Let's listen in. . . .

Advisor: What's new in your life? Any recent vacations?

Prospect: Yes, just came back from a terrific golf trip with seven of my old college buddies. Eight days playing the best courses in Scotland. It was glorious!

Advisor: Yeah? Where did you play?

Prospect: Gleneagles, Turnberry, Troon . . .

Advisor (interrupting): I love Troon, played it several years ago myself! How about that third hole! Was the wind a big factor when you played it? When I was there, the wind was gusting over 60 miles an hour and the rain was coming in sideways and . . .

What is going on? Why did the advisor feel the need to interrupt? It's the "big dog effect" at work; he's essentially saying, "I'm successful, too! I've been to Scotland, too!" Do prospects and clients care, or are they instead more interested in someone who focuses attention on them? Don't most people long for someone to just be interested in them? It's hard to apply empathy and empathic communication if one is absorbed in self-orientation.

The Application of Empathy and Empathic Communication

At the conclusion of Chapter 4, we described four vignettes of negative scripts and asked how you might respond to each. Let's begin with Mary, a 71-year-old widow whose husband Harry died five years ago and left her a sizable equity portfolio. Although the income is no longer adequate to support her lifestyle, she refuses to modify her portfolio, contending, "Harry told me to never touch the stocks."

We raised the question, "If Mary were my client, how would I approach her, what would I say and do so that she will be receptive to altering her current view, a view that may be difficult to change since it represents her husband's dying wishes?" In essence, Mary was bound by a powerful script authored by her well-intentioned, late husband. Unfortunately, Harry's best intentions were now working against Mary's adopting a more viable financial plan because she felt that such a move would disrespect the memory of her late husband.

Let's examine the actions of a Charismatic Advisor, whom we will call Janice, and her thoughts about approaching Mary. Janice attempted to place herself in Mary's shoes, appreciating that in any meeting they had there would be a strong elephant in the room — Harry and his dying wishes. Janice understood that ignoring this elephant would render any recommendations fruitless. No amount of logical reasoning backed by financial charts and statistics would change Mary's position as long as the elephant was not addressed. But how? With this in mind, consider the following possible dialogue:

Janice says, "In everything you've told me about Harry, it sounds as if he was a very caring, loving husband, and one of his strongest wishes was to make certain you were financially secure when he died. He didn't want you to have any worries about living a comfortable lifestyle."

Mary agrees.

Janice continues, "I want to bring up some thoughts I have about your financial holdings, but before I do there is something I want to say. If at any point you feel anything I say is not being respectful of Harry, please let me know since that is not my intention at all."

This last comment is a vivid illustration of empathic communication. Janice skillfully identified the elephant in the room and invited Mary to let her know if anything she says is disrespectful of Harry.

Mary, perhaps sensing that Janice will suggest changes in her portfolio, responds, "I appreciate your saying that, but I know that Harry wanted what is best for me and that's why he said not to sell any of my stocks."

Janice replies, "I'm glad you put it that way. As I mentioned, I think Harry wanted the best for you. But what I was thinking of is that when Harry told you not to sell any of your stocks, he was doing so based on the best information he had at that time. I know that if he were alive today he would still have the same wish of wanting to make certain you're financially secure, but perhaps his recommendations would be different. So much has happened in the markets during the past five years that Harry couldn't have imagined or predicted."

Mary answers, "That's certainly true. Some of the stocks and funds that seemed so safe when Harry was alive are losing money right now."

"You're right," Janice responds. "I think Harry would have recognized that it would not be advantageous for you to sell shares of companies at such depressed values in order to meet your ongoing cash flow needs. I may be wrong, but I think that, if Harry were here, he would consider changes in your overall strategy."

What we have just presented may seem like an "ideal" dialogue, but when advisors engage in empathic communication, there is more of a chance to have a constructive discussion with a client than when empathy is limited. Some may wonder how Janice might have responded had Mary continued to say, "I feel like I'm being disrespectful to Harry if I go against his suggestions." Perhaps Janice would then have the liberty to "invite" Harry into the discussion. Janice might then ask, "Mary, I'm glad you can tell me how you feel, but I'm wondering what Harry might say if he were with us today and seeing all that we see. Do you think he might agree that we need to ensure that you continue to have enough income to meet your needs?"

This kind of dialogue might open Mary's eyes to an expanded way of thinking about Harry's vision and how it relates to today's realities. Of course, deep-seated perspectives are not changed overnight. Bob has found in his clinical work that it takes time for many of us to process a different way of perceiving things. After presenting a new idea in therapy that is not readily embraced by a patient, Bob will say, "I know you might not be certain about the idea I just presented, but I think it's worth thinking about and something we can talk more about during the next few weeks." This comment validates the patient's perspective but also serves to keep the issue open for further consideration.

Of course, as advisors (or therapists, such as Bob) we must be prepared for the possibility that even our most empathic statements may not lead to the cooperative attitude we desire. However, empathy will increase the probability of developing more satisfying, trusting relationships.

Two of the other vignettes described at the end of the last chapter, involving Susan and William and Jill and Jack, have many features in common, including marriages replete with stress, and issues of accusations and blame related to finances.

Financial advisors often feel like marital counselors when confronted with such couples. As David has written with Alan Parisse in the book *Questions Great Financial Advisors Ask and Investors Need to Know*, many couples bring a unique history or set of baggage to the table when it comes to their view of money, and rarely is it a matching set. As David and Alan discuss, a vital dimension of an advisor's role is dealing with the underlying "investment wiring" of clients. Few advisors are trained to be marital counselors, but perhaps we can learn something by probing into these two vignettes a bit further to appreciate how practicing empathy and empathic communication might be of value.

Empathy and Empathic Communication

Bob has learned when conducting marital therapy that there are numerous land mines to avoid, especially being sensitive to either spouse's feeling that Bob is aligning with the other spouse. Empathy toward both members of the couple is essential. As we suggested when working with Mary, elephants in the room must be identified. Also, if you are to assume the role of a Charismatic Advisor, you must use empathic communication to reinforce a basic principle of resilience; namely, problems represent opportunities for problem solving (also a key feature of stress hardiness).

It's not unusual for husbands and wives each to elicit your support for their position. However, taking sides is fraught with danger. Thus, with Susan and William or Jill and Jack, parameters need to be established when a spouse asks implicitly or explicitly for your support against the other. An empathic comment might be, "I see that you both have different views of what has contributed to your financial situation and that your worries have sometimes led to blaming each other. The role I would like to serve is to help you find solutions to the problems you've mentioned and to make certain that each of you feels you are able to express your view without any worries of being criticized."

In his therapy work Bob frequently adds, "I find that sometimes one spouse wants me to side with his or her position against the other. I am not here to take sides but rather to bring people together. Thus, if at any time I feel you are asking me to wear a black robe and assume the role of a judge, I will let you know since I am not here to be a judge and render a decision. I am here to help you find solutions."

Bob often continues, "If either of you ever feels I have put on the robe, please let me know."

Let's try to extend some of this theory a bit further to the case of Susan and William. As introduced in the last chapter, Susan is married to William. William makes a very good, but not spectacular, income. No matter how much Susan and William accumulate in the way of assets, Susan always feels poor. She constantly reminds William of what she perceives to be their precarious financial existence. Her financial insecurity impacts William's sense of personal success, which reinforces his own feelings of failure, often paralyzing him from taking realistic risks. A vicious cycle operates to maintain a negative script.

Most advisors may feel very unprepared to grapple with the issues surrounding Susan and William's marriage, including Susan's strong sense of insecurity. Yet, in advising Susan and William about their finances it is impossible to avoid the negative scripts that characterize their relationship. Think about how best to approach this couple.

Janice observes, "I sense there is clearly some tension here surrounding your financial situation."

William responds, "I think we're doing just fine."

Susan disagrees, "Well, I don't!! Our friends are doing so much better than we are! I have no idea how we'll ever be able to afford to retire."

Janice interjects, "I'd like to take on the role here of dispassionate observer. Would it be okay for me to give you some completely objective feedback to what you have shown me regarding your financial picture?"

"Sure, I would *love* to hear it," replies Susan as William nods.

Janice continues, "As we work together I want to emphasize that over the past 20 years I have had the privilege of providing financial advice to many families such as yours. Although I limit my practice to 150 families, over the years I have met with well over 1,000 households and have had the opportunity to 'peek under the hood' and gain an understanding of their financial footings. I've certainly learned that the needs of each family are very different, and one has to be careful not to make comparisons among families based on their income and wealth. My job is to help you identify your financial needs and the resources you require to meet these needs."

William says, "I agree, and I think that's where you can be of help to Susan and me. I get upset because I feel Susan thinks we are heading for welfare, and that makes me feel like I've let her down."

Susan jumps in. "Well, I do worry about our future. But when we try to talk about my worries, you immediately feel I'm criticizing you for not making a higher salary or investing better."

"Well, it certainly comes across as criticism to me, almost as if you're saying, 'If you were a better breadwinner, we could live much more comfortably.'"

Janice listens closely and says, "I've had a chance to review the financial material you sent me. It was very helpful. What I hope is that our discussion will provide a much clearer picture of your finances and ease some of the worries and tension that exist. Also, I want to concentrate on your situation and not on that of your friends or neighbors. I've learned that what you see on the outside may not be a very good indicator of another family's financial health. As a matter of fact, I often recommend a book by Thomas Stanley and William Danko, *The Millionaire Next Door.* They look at how often the people with significant money are those you would least expect to have accumulated as much as they have."

Susan says, "I think someone else told me about that book, but William and I haven't read it."

Janice replies, "You might want to at some point. Also, if you look statistically at the country as a whole, William's income puts him in the top 3 percent of all wage earners. Finally, as I look at your financial situation and compare you to the 1,000-plus households I've interacted with over the years, you're doing pretty well and are on your way to financial independence, as long as prudent choices are made moving forward. If we are to proceed together, my role will be to call it the way I see it and to join together with both of you to achieve the goal of financial independence for your future."

What has Janice accomplished? Did she take sides? Did she cross the line from financial advisor into marriage counselor? We think not. We believe she exemplified how a Charismatic Advisor can use empathy and empathic communication to rise to the top of the water and not get mired down amid the weeds. First, she positioned herself as a dispassionate observer by implying that she's not going to take sides. Second, she asked permission to provide her unvarnished opinion, always a good idea when we find ourselves in delicate conversations. Third, she played to her strengths as a financial expert, much the way an expert witness gets positioned in court, and provided some objective "supporting evidence" about William and Susan's financial situation. Finally, she joined together with them surrounding the common goal of financial independence.

Without confronting the vicious cycle that William and Susan have scripted, Janice may help to break it nonetheless. She has tackled three important elephants: Susan's fear of poverty, her perception of the financial prowess of her friends, and William's feelings of insecurity. Such negative scripts are not easily cast aside, but perhaps over time Janice's support will help Susan and William replace them with the positive script of being on the road to financial independence and working more effectively together as a couple.

Another empathic approach with couples who are quick to blame or accuse each other is to introduce what is called the "exception rule" in solution-focused therapy. An application of this rule for financial advisors is to ask the couple if they can think of times when they were able to discuss finances without anger or blame entering the dialogue. When Bob uses the exception rule in his clinical practice, he finds that almost every couple can think about a time they did interact more cooperatively. He then asks the couple to reflect upon what in the particular situation contributed to this more cooperative stance so they might use the information in future conversations.

If a couple reply that they cannot think of a time they were able to speak in a more civil, less accusatory manner with each other, Bob's response is to ask if they would like to learn how. All respond in the affirmative, which permits a problem to be turned into a problem-solving activity.

Although financial advisors are not therapists, you can apply the exception rule in furthering a constructive dialogue with couples who are your clients. How might the exception rule apply to the case of Jill and Jack? Remember, they have been married for 30 years and rarely agree about how to invest their money.

Again, let's turn to Janice as our advisor.

Jill explains, "Whatever decisions we make with our money are *always* wrong. Actually, they are more Jack's decisions than mine, since he feels that I don't know much about finances. He gives me no credit for having some intelligence."

Jack counters, "That's not true!"

Jill responds, "You don't see it that way, but it is true."

The argument continues for a while, and Janice recognizes that it is not going down a productive path. She decides to use the exception rule.

"Can either of you remember a financial decision that you made together that turned out right?"

Without hesitating Jill emphatically says, "Never!"

Janice asks, "Never?"

Jack says, "I can remember that early on in our marriage we decided to save up for a piece of property on the shore. That was a great financial decision."

Jill agrees. "It sure was! That property has appreciated twenty-fold. And that was one time I felt that Jack asked for and listened to my opinion."

Janice responds, "You know, it might be very helpful to reflect on the collaborative spirit that led to that great financial decision and see how we might be able to bring that approach to other decision making."

This kind of empathic dialogue, prompted by the exception rule, can lead to more successful interactions with our clients and help us become Charismatic Advisors in their lives.

The fourth vignette involved Joseph, a 62-year-old physician who was feeling burned out, and his wife, Samantha. The latter voiced concern about her husband's retiring. "He can't retire; he has no hobbies — he won't know what to do with himself." However, their financial advisor sensed that Samantha's comments were rooted in anxieties about their net worth and whether they could really afford to have Joseph retire.

How might you introduce what you believe to be Samantha's true worry without having her feel you are trying to read her mind and prompting defensiveness and annoyance on her part? Empathic communication is essential in handling this delicate situation. The following statement represents one approach you can use; it includes a validation of Samantha's stated position but also offers an opening to explore her unstated worries:

"Samantha, one problem that some people have when they retire is not really knowing what to do with their time. I see this with many clients. They haven't spent enough time considering what they truly enjoy doing. This is something that you and Joseph should certainly discuss. You can think about things you enjoy doing by yourself and what you would enjoy doing as a couple.

"As your financial advisor I want to bring up another concern that most couples have at retirement. They worry about whether or not they have enough financial resources to support the lifestyle they would like to lead. Perhaps we can step back and visualize life in retirement in order to craft a hypothetical budget. This will help us look realistically at what you feel you will need in retirement and how your finances will meet those needs."

Samantha will be much more open to engaging in a discussion about her *real* worries if Janice first validates the concerns she's expressed, even if her concerns about Joseph's having no hobbies represent a smokescreen. Also, the way Janice introduced worries about finances is housed within a problem-solving approach, lessening feelings of fear and helplessness.

Empathy: A Concluding Thought

Being empathic and using empathic communication are essential ingredients for developing a trusting, caring relationship. Such positive features serve as the foundation for the creation of what we call a "motivating environment," an environment in which our clients are genuinely motivated to work with us in a collaborative fashion. In the next chapter we will highlight the concept of motivating environments and will identify key components that encourage the development of such environments.

Reflections

Consider the last time a client asked, "How are you doing?" Such a question is not unusual during or in the immediate aftermath of difficult markets. Consider for a few moments how you might respond and why you might respond in that way.

Obviously, your answer will be based in great part on your relationship with your client and your empathic understanding of why the client has asked you the question. Is the client concerned about the pressure and stress you might be experiencing? Are you communicating uncertainty and anxiety, which may be reinforcing the client's own level of distress? In a seemingly caring way, is the client expressing dissatisfaction with your handling of his or her finances?

As an advisor you may not be clear about the intentions of the client, but reflect upon and be guided by a couple of the questions we raised about empathic communication; namely:

- In anything I say or do, what do I hope to accomplish?
- Am I saying or doing things in a manner in which other people will be most responsive to listening to what I have to say?

How would these questions assist you in replying to your client? If a key goal is to reinforce a collaborative, trusting relationship with your client, when you are asked, "How are you doing?" it is important not to confide about your own financial life but to reply with a problem-solving attitude such as, "Thanks for asking. It's been a challenging time for advisors and clients alike, yet I am gratified that so many of our clients continue to place their confidence in us and appreciate that together we are getting through this very difficult period."

Think about other situations you have encountered as an advisor and the ways in which empathy and empathic communication will enrich your interactions with clients.

CHAPTER 6

Creating "Motivating Environments": The Roots of Collaboration

In his clinical practice and workshops, Bob is frequently asked questions about motivation. Here are some samples, which we are certain sound familiar to all our readers.

- "How do I motivate my daughter to clean her room?"
- "How do I motivate my son to do his homework?"
- "The only motivation that gets my kid to do what I want him to do is to ground him and take away computer time. But this only seems to work temporarily. Is there a better approach?"
- "How do I motivate my staff to do their work more conscientiously and effectively?"
- "I work for a boss who always tells me what to do, but his constant reminders make me angry. Is that the way to motivate staff?"
- "I'm a high school teacher. Students today just don't seem as interested in doing their homework or term papers. What can I do to motivate them to meet these class requirements?"
- "How do I motivate my husband to spend more time with our kids?"

In David's work coaching advisors, the questions often parallel those Bob hears:

- "I want to be more proactive serving existing clients and attracting new clients relationships, but I can't seem to find the time. What can I do?"
- "How can I get more prospects to meet with me?"
- "How can I more effectively motivate prospects to abandon the status quo and move forward with plans I propose?"

Creating "Motivating Environments"

Obviously, the list of questions pertaining to motivation can go on and on. Years ago, given the frequency and saliency of these questions from spouses, parents, teachers, and business people, Bob introduced the concept of "motivating environments." He posed the following question:

"How do we create environments in which others feel safe and secure and desire to work with us even when confronted with challenging tasks or challenging times?" Stated somewhat differently, "How do we create environments that nurture motivation and collaboration rather than inertia and mistrust?"

Some answers to these questions may be found in our previous discussions of applying empathy and empathic communication and nurturing trust. It's a monumental task to create motivating environments when clients don't feel heard or understood, when they have doubts about how genuine and sincere we are, and when they feel we're not accessible or available. Under these conditions clients are more likely to use what has been termed "avoidance motivation," a concept we'll refer to again in the next chapter. As the term "avoidance" implies, this kind of motivation finds expression in clients' distancing themselves from us and having little, if any, desire to work with us.

There are advisors who are skilled in creating motivating environments by establishing and maintaining a collaborative relationship with their clients — they display empathy and garner trust. Advisors such as John Rafal, Lori Van Dusen, Augie Cenname, Rebecca Rothstein, and Todd Silaika, all of whom we mentioned earlier in this book, are skillful architects in designing and implementing motivating environments. Below are some guiding principles to consider if you are to become similarly skilled.

Deci's Focus on Basic Needs

Bob has found the work of psychologist Edward Deci at the University of Rochester to provide a practical and realistic framework that can be applied in numerous situations to nurture the development of a motivating environment. Deci's work, which is similar to a model advanced by psychiatrist William Glaser, assumes as a basic premise that each of us has particular needs. When these needs are satisfied in a systematic, consistent manner by others, the seeds for a motivating environment are planted. When these needs are not met, people are less likely to be cooperative or to want to work with us.

In his workshops for teachers, Bob has emphasized that their first responsibilities are not to teach a particular subject matter but rather to make certain that each student feels as safe, secure, and trusting as possible. Relying on Deci's framework, Bob has said that students will have these positive feelings when their needs have been met. In such a climate students will be more eager to learn from and respect teachers.

A parallel situation exists for financial advisors. If clients feel you care about them and are accessible and collaborative, you have created a motivating environment in which your clients are more likely to trust you with their assets and be comfortable working with you.

Deci posits three basic needs. As we review them, reflect upon the extent to which you meet these needs in your clients. Also, think about people in your personal or professional life with whom you are motivated to collaborate and those with whom you're not. What are the differences between these two groups?

The need to belong and feel connected. Certainly, clients want to feel that we're experts in our profession. They won't want to work with someone who lacks the skills to perform competently, whether as a financial advisor, a psychologist, a surgeon, or a hairdresser. However, more is involved in creating a motivating environment than the degree or certificate initials that follow our names. Clients want to feel we care about them, that they are not simply *clients* whose money we manage. Clients want to feel that we know who they are. They want to know that when they call we will return the call within a reasonable time.

Maurice and Sonia Brill decided that they needed a financial advisor. They asked close friends for possible recommendations, but all except two said they didn't use an advisor. Interestingly, though, most said they probably should. One friend remarked, "I would give you my advisor's name, but quite honestly, I'm thinking of switching advisors. I feel I'm always chasing him instead of his initiating discussions. Also, sometimes it takes him a couple of days to get back to me. When he finally calls he apologizes and tells me how busy he is, especially with all of his clients being so worried about their portfolios. He always seems so hurried."

The other friend who recommended an advisor to Maurice and Sonia was very enthusiastic about making a referral. "He's always on top of things. He will check in with us on a regular basis. He really knows how to connect with people. When we call and he's busy, he always finds out when we'll be free to speak with him. We know he has many clients, but we never feel rushed, and he takes time to answer all our questions."

The notion of belonging and feeling connected with Charismatic Advisors runs deep. Maurice and Sonia's friends most likely felt a profound sense of connectivity to their advisor because they believe he truly cares about their well-being. It's not enough to feel a sense of belonging if it's not deeply rooted. Charismatic Advisors provide a sincere sense that they have the client's "back" at all times, that they are connected, "shoulder to shoulder," as the primary advocate for the client's core financial priorities.

Is it little wonder that Maurice and Sonia called this second advisor?

When people feel a lack of connection to a teacher, a therapist, or any other professional, they are less likely to want to work with and cooperate with that professional. Interestingly, several years ago Harvard Medical School made substantial changes in their curriculum for medical students, changes that involved training medical students to gain a more thorough understanding of illness from the patient's perspective. One way to do this was for medical students to shadow patients to their different appointments, actually spending time with them in waiting rooms and chatting about nonmedical issues.

The former dean at Harvard Medical School, Dr. Joseph Martin, was a major force in initiating changes in the curriculum. He was concerned that students were perceiving patients as "cases" when "it's all about patients as people. We want to create a different mindset." A *Time* magazine article written by Nathan Thornburgh described the changes at Harvard Medical School. He wrote, "Why would the U.S.'s top medical school ask its students to spend valuable time trailing a patient instead of a doctor? At Harvard and other medical school across the country, educators are beginning to realize that empathy is as valuable to a doctor as any clinical skill. Whether it's acknowledging that a patient was inconvenienced by having to wait an hour before being seen or listening when someone explains why he didn't take meds, doctors who try to understand their patients may be the best antidote for the widespread dissatisfaction with today's health care system."

The worlds of the medical student and the financial advisor may seem far apart, but the concept of seeing patients or clients as people and connecting with them in a meaningful way has much in common in both professions. As we have emphasized, trust is built when clients feel we genuinely care about them. When trust is established, it's a sturdy scaffolding for the creation of a motivating environment.

In Chapter 3 we described the three dimensions of trust that David highlights in his workshops around the country with advisors and discusses in his book *This Is Your Time* (coauthored with Alan Parisse, third edition released in 2009). The first dimension of trust, the visceral dimension, relates squarely to the discussion in this chapter. Charismatic Advisors rarely have a problem with getting clients to *want* to have a deep connection to them once they pass the visceral dimension of trust. The visceral dimension quite simply gets to the core question, "Do I like you?" Augie Cenname comes to mind as the perfect example here. If you have the pleasure of meeting Augie someday, his laser focus on you will have you liking him immediately; when Augie meets you it's as if you are the only person on the planet. Clients feel connected to Augie and enjoy a sense of belonging to his exclusive club.

The need for self-determination and autonomy. Have you ever been in a situation in which you were told what to do without the opportunity to voice your opinion or raise questions? If you have, how did it feel? Even when meeting with a professional whose expertise in an area far exceeds our own, as typically occurs in a physician-patient relationship, we still want to feel that we have a major voice in determining decisions about treatment options. While we welcome the recommendations of the physician, we want our voice to he heard. When people experience others as not respecting or honoring their viewpoint, they are less likely to be cooperative.

The Charismatic Advisor

As we emphasized in earlier chapters, a Charismatic Advisor is one who invites collaboration. The hard sell of Larry, whom we met in Chapter 3, did not fare well with his clients. Larry's mindset was predicated on the belief that once he presented his data, it would be a mistake for a client not to comply with his recommendations. In describing Larry's approach, we noted that he's quick to minimize or dismiss questions raised by his clients, not necessarily in a rude way but in a manner that suggests, "I am the expert here; just follow my lead."

We contrasted Larry's style with that of Ian. They were both experts in market fluctuations, but Ian invited discussion and encouraged clients to ask questions. Ian recognized that clients would be more motivated to work with him if he openly recognized the collaborative nature of his relationship with them. He did so with such comments as these:

- "If I present any material that's not clear, please let me know."
- "Never think that any question you have is too simple or too silly."
- "Before we make any decisions about changes in your portfolio, I'd like to make certain that you feel comfortable doing so and that I've answered any questions you might have."
- "I view our relationship as a partnership."

Ian created a motivating environment by appreciating the importance of meeting the client's need for self-determination. As you might guess, this need relates directly to a sense of personal control, a major component of stress hardiness. When people feel they have little say over what is transpiring in their lives, personal control is thwarted, and people tend to become angry and less receptive to working with the individuals who they perceive are denying them any choice.

A lack of collaboration and personal control not only serves as a barrier to the formation of a motivating environment, but it can also have a significant impact on the health of individuals, further lessening their commitment and motivation to work with us. Having control over one's life appears to be a basic drive for all human beings. Research supports the importance of personal control as a major force in emotional and physical well-being.

Creating "Motivating Environments"

As an example, an article published in the *Boston Globe* in July 1997 reported a study published in the British journal *Lancet*. The research, conducted by Michael Marmot of University College in London, found that it was not senior executives who were more likely to die of heart attacks but rather their clerks and secretaries. Even taking into consideration such variables as smoking and poor nutrition, the researchers found that the "lower the job category and the less the control," the more likely people were to suffer from heart disease.

Marmot's group noted, "Greater attention to the design of work environments may be one important way to reduce inequalities in health." Others concurred, noting that it was probably easier to provide people more control at work than to change their social status. Leonard Syme and Jennifer Balfour, commenting on the Marmot study, contended, "Although it may be difficult to intervene on social class inequalities in health, there are more opportunities to intervene on control. It may also be possible to change environmental forces in the workplace or the community so that more flexibility and control is available."

Similar findings to those of Marmot were reported by Laura Kubansky, a researcher at the Harvard School of Public Health. Kubansky, taking into account such risk factors for heart disease as smoking, high cholesterol, blood pressure, drinking, and family history, found that men in their 60s were less likely to develop coronary heart disease if they possessed an optimistic outlook on life. She noted, "This shows again there's a link between how people look at the world and what happens to them physically. This also shows that optimism can be protective." A major component of optimism was reported to be the belief that the future will be more pleasant because, to a great extent, we can control important events in our lives.

The need to feel competent. When Bob first became familiar with Edward Deci's framework, he was thrilled to see the word "competent" included in the third need. For almost 30 years Bob has used a metaphor in his work to highlight the strength-based approach to which he subscribes. He has said that we all have "islands of competence." As we noted in the Introduction, Bob's early training and clinical activities focused primarily on a person's weaknesses and vulnerabilities, and far too often lip service was given to that individual's strengths. When almost all of a person's energy is directed toward examining what is wrong with another person, there is little opportunity to identify and reinforce the beauty and strength of each individual.

In his initial session with patients of any age, Bob not only gathers information about the problems for which they are seeking help for themselves (or in the case of parents for their children), he asks them about their strengths (or the strengths of their kids). He has found that some patients have focused on their perceived weaknesses and shortcomings for such a long time that they have difficulty identifying their interests and competencies.

When Bob first began to ask patients about their strengths, he thought they would be eager to respond and enthusiastically describe their strong points and interests — and some did. But to those who said, "I don't know what my strengths are," Bob asked if they would like to figure out what they enjoyed doing and what they thought they did rather well. Invariably, the answer was "yes." At that point Bob turned the interaction into a problem-solving, collaborative effort by emphasizing, "Together, we can try to figure out what you [or in the case of parents, "what you and your children"] like to do and do rather well."

How might a financial advisor satisfy his clients' need to feel competent and in the process create a motivating environment? One of the most obvious ways ties to the previous need for self-determination. Advisors can find genuine ways of communicating that their clients possess insights and knowledge that are invaluable in developing an effective financial plan. Review the comments earlier in this chapter that Ian expressed toward his clients. Not only was he reinforcing a collaborative relationship, but he was also communicating a respect for his client's abilities. More direct statements might include some like these:

- "Your insights and input are invaluable, especially since you already have a good sense of your financial goals."
- "I'm impressed with the thinking you've done about your financial needs and your risk tolerance. Your preparation makes it easier for us to consider how you would like to

position your portfolio and provide for your grandchildren's college education."

- "I see you've done some thinking about what you would enjoy doing once the two of you are retired, and it sounds like you have a good idea of what will bring you a lot of pleasure. I really want to help you reach those goals and dreams."

This last comment relates to another avenue through which you as an advisor can meet your clients' need to feel competent. We've emphasized that in developing trust advisors must display a genuine caring for clients. This caring can be enhanced by asking your clients such questions as these:

- "Outside work, what do you enjoy doing?"
- "Of all your activities which ones do you feel most confident about? What do you see as your strengths? I ask about strengths and interests because I often see people who get so caught up with work and even family responsibilities that they don't set aside even a little time for doing things they enjoy and that bring a sense of accomplishment. As your advisor I want to protect you from falling into that trap. Also, the more I know about your strengths and interests, the more we can plan on your having the financial freedom to engage in them."

Think about all the important messages communicated in this last paragraph. Caring is enhanced when clients feel we appreciate their strengths.

Bob recalls attending a soccer game of one of his adolescent patients and the school plays of two others; they wanted Bob to witness their islands of competence in action. A woman patient, whom Bob had encouraged to spend time painting, an activity she described as a "true love" and one that she found very satisfying, gave Bob one of her paintings as a token of her appreciation when treatment ended.

Try the following activity: Make a list of all of your clients and what they perceive as their islands of competence. If you're not certain, ask them the next time you see them. Think about ways to introduce these strengths into your discussions with them about their financial goals and ways to express your appreciation of those strengths.

Ian's clients, Tyler and Melissa, talked about Tyler's love of sailing and his expertise in this activity. Melissa raved about how her husband had helped to build their boat. She also talked about how much they enjoy sailing and how they hoped they would have more time to do it, especially when they retire.

Not only did Ian ask them to bring in photos of the boat, which they were thrilled to do, but he also asked Tyler questions about building the boat. He then said that, as he considered their financial plans, he would take into consideration their desire to have more time for sailing. He added, "It's wonderful when people can do what brings them so much enjoyment. And it's obvious, Tyler, that building and sailing the boat are areas of real satisfaction and strength for you."

When clients believe that financial advisors understand not only their concerns and worries but their strengths as well, they are more likely to enter into a long-term relationship with that advisor — the relationship is housed within a motivating environment.

Understanding Coping Strategies and "Avoidance Motivation"

Even as we attempt to meet the three needs outlined by Deci, it is not always an easy task to create motivating environments with our clients. Obstacles appear. One of the most formidable roadblocks involves the different coping strategies used by clients to deal with their anxieties, some of which involve avoiding our input and recommendations. The skillful use of empathy and empathic communication will be paramount in lessening so-called "avoidance motivation" and managing those coping styles that interfere with the emergence of a motivating environment. We turn our attention to the theme of coping strategies in the next chapter.

Reflections

Write a list of your top 20 client relationships. Can you identify the "islands of competence" for each client?

The financial advisory community's support in retirement planning sometimes focuses too much on the numbers. Charismatic Advisors discover each client's passion and her unique "islands of competence" and then seek to help her embrace such passions in anticipation of her retirement years. Even if clients are several years from retirement, consider starting to engage them in conversations surrounding how they visualize life in retirement. Perhaps there are actions they should be taking today in light of such desires.

Take Dan, a 57-year-old senior executive, with a core "island of competence" in mentoring others. Upon discussion with his advisor, Dan realized that he could channel his expertise and passion for mentoring into a "next career" upon retirement, by teaching at a college in the community where he and his wife plan to relocate. This led Dan's advisor to motivate him to start writing articles in trade journals and to start teaching in the evenings at a local college. Dan is now considering writing a book.

CHAPTER 7

Understanding Client *Coping Strategies:* A Path to Lessening Defensiveness and Nurturing Motivation

Years ago, when his sons were playing in Little League, Bob observed the reactions of two nine-year-old boys on one of his son's teams when they each struck out the two times they were at bat in the game. Jeremy approached the coach at the end of the game and said, "Coach, I'm striking out a lot. I'm not sure why. Maybe you can watch me and see if you can spot something. I think I can hit better than I have been hitting."

Seth, a teammate of Jeremy's, responded very differently after striking out. Displaying noticeable frustration and anger, he threw his bat and helmet on the ground and screamed at the umpire, "You're blind, blind, blind! If you weren't so blind, I wouldn't strike out so much." To the consternation and embarrassment of his parents, Seth ran into a wooded area adjacent to the field and could not be coaxed to continue playing.

Three high school friends, Grace, Barry, and Alyssa, just received their scores on a math test they took the previous week. None of them did very well. Grace said to Barry and Alyssa, "I thought I knew the material, but I guess it's still not very clear to me. I'm going to go to the teacher and get extra help."

Barry retorted, "Why should you go for extra help? It's not our fault we didn't do well on the test. The teacher is lousy. I would never go to that teacher for extra help."

Alyssa chimed in, "I wouldn't go for extra help, either, but not because I think the teacher is a lousy teacher. I just can't understand math. I've always had trouble with math. All the tutoring in the world won't help, especially as the math keeps getting more and more difficult. I'm a math retard."

Remember financial advisors Staci and Andrew? In response to the downturn in the market, Andrew grew increasingly sad and anxious. He became obsessed with watching CNBC and failed to return the phone calls of his clients. In contrast, Staci was proactive, initiating contact with her clients, reviewing their portfolios. She also made certain she exercised and ate properly.

Coping Strategies: Effective and Ineffective

Jeremy, Seth, Grace, Barry, Alyssa, Staci, and Andrew all demonstrate different ways of coping with challenging events. We all use coping strategies on a daily basis to deal with challenging situations. Some forms of coping are effective, leading to personal growth and mastery of problems. For example, clients cope positively when they don't panic, when they don't blame themselves or you as their advisor for the decreased value of their portfolio. Rather, they engage in a thoughtful dialogue with you, obtaining information and reviewing different options to deal with an uncertain, even turbulent, market.

Not surprisingly, advisors, like their clients, also display various coping strategies. As we highlighted in Chapter 2, advisors who practice stress hardiness avoid blaming themselves or others. Instead, they accept responsibility for how they manage the challenges that confront them.

Unfortunately, as illustrated by the responses of Seth, Barry, Alyssa, and Andrew, some coping techniques prove self-defeating and counterproductive. They actually exacerbate, rather than ameliorate, the situation. Little, if any, growth transpires when people blame others, when they make excuses, when they have outbursts, when they quit, or when they refuse to attempt certain tasks.

Why would people resort to ineffective coping strategies? Remember that such strategies are called into action to deal with situations that are perceived to be difficult, even threatening to an individual's sense of security. When people experience their problems as overwhelming and not open to solutions, they rely on coping behaviors that carry them away from a constructive course of action.

It's important to recognize that people may not even appreciate the extent to which their coping behaviors are self-defeating and that these behaviors intensify, rather then relieve, stress. It's as if they subscribe to the attitude: "If I can't fix it, why even attempt it and aggravate myself even more?" Sadly, if they don't confront these difficult events constructively, their aggravation is likely to intensify.

Coping with Coping Strategies

In our interactions with clients, we witness a wide spectrum of coping maneuvers, as we saw in the case examples described in earlier chapters. A key question if we are to be Charismatic Advisors is how to respond to the various coping styles of our clients, especially those that become obstacles to our working collaboratively with them. If we're going to be successful, we must make sure that our own ways of coping are realistic, proactive, and effective. We need to practice empathy by recognizing and responding to our clients' different coping strategies and appreciate that these coping strategies, regardless of how effective or ineffective we judge them to be, serve a purpose for each client.

In our meetings with clients, we advisors can initiate a discussion about coping strategies, using the principles of empathic communication we discussed in Chapter 5 to make sure that clients don't perceive such a discussion as a criticism of their behaviors.

Advisors may open the discussion of the client's main coping strategies by asking in a caring way, "How do you typically handle things when the market and your portfolio are going down?"

If the client seems unsure as to how to answer, an advisor might say, "I've found that my clients react in different ways to a downturn in the market. Some may avoid looking at the market or reviewing their portfolio, while others constantly evaluate and modify their financial picture. It's helpful for me to know what you find most beneficial when dealing with stressful events. As your advisor I will also let you know what I think will work best for you, but I'll always welcome your observations and input."

This statement sets the tone for the advisor to achieve two major goals. First, she is careful not to state which coping strategies she finds effective and which she judges to be self-defeating. Many people use their coping strategies as a shield to ward off danger, so an advisor's attempts to strip away a client's shield too abruptly can lead the client to employ an even stronger shield, which can severely compromise the relationship.

A second main goal is to highlight the collaborative nature of the advisor-client relationship. One cannot be a Charismatic Advisor in the absence of true collaboration, rooted in a sense of caring, respect, and trust.

The following represent a sampling of the wide spectrum of coping techniques that clients experience:

- "I don't open statements or read the business news. Why aggravate myself?"
- "I watch CNBC as constantly as I can. I have to keep up with what's happening. I don't want to miss advice about buying a particular stock or investing in a certain sector."
- "I become angry. Sometimes I'm angry with myself for not anticipating the latest market downturn and repositioning my portfolio. Sometimes I'm angry with my financial advisor for not predicting the downturn. All I know is that I've lost a lot of money."
- "I look for the opportunities that may exist in such a depressed market."
- "I try not to worry too much. I'm not retiring for at least 10 years and feel that if past history is any predictor of the future, the market will come back. Also, I keep in regular touch with my advisor so we can review my allocations to see if any changes are indicated."
- "I cry as I watch my hard-earned money go down the drain. I wish the crying would relieve some of the stress and sadness I feel, but it doesn't. I'm feeling more and more anxious. I don't know when I've felt this scared."
- "I try to find comforting things to do. It's so therapeutic to go to a movie with my wife, especially a comedy. Also, when I'm playing with my young grandkids and one of them gives me a hug and says, 'Grandpa, I love you,' it's as if the world's problems disappear. I know the problems are still there, but the 'I love you' puts things in perspective for me."

There are so many ways clients perceive and respond to difficult situations. Some demonstrate stress hardiness in their approach, while others fall prey to the ravages of stress.

Advisor, Know Thyself

Earlier in this chapter we wrote that to be successful as an advisor you need to make sure that the ways you choose to cope are realistic, proactive, and effective. Knowing what your own preferred ways of coping are will not only help you deal more successfully with the responses of your clients but can be the basis for modifying those parts of your own behavior that may keep you from becoming a Charismatic Advisor.

In their book *Primal Leadership: Realizing the Power of Emotional Intelligence*, Daniel Goleman, Richard Boyatzis, and Annie McKee highlighted self-awareness as a key dimension of emotional intelligence. They defined self-awareness this way:

"Simply put, self-awareness means having a deep understanding of one's emotions, as well as one's strengths and limitations and one's values and motives. People with strong self-awareness are realistic — neither overly self-critical nor naively hopeful. Rather, they are honest with themselves about themselves. . . . Self-aware leaders also understand their values, goals and dreams."

On the surface, you might wonder, "Aren't most people aware of their emotions and the ways in which they express these emotions? Aren't they aware of how others experience their behavior?" As we touched upon in our discussion of empathy, some people do display a limited understanding of how they come across to others. Also, some are trapped by negative scripts and fail to realize the different options they have for coping with challenging events.

For example, in a consultation Bob conducted for a national firm, he was asked to focus on a particular department with a high turnover rate. In exit interviews several departing staff described the manager of the department as "angry," "easily upset," "unpredictable," "scary," and "a yeller." One person said, "You never know what to expect. One moment he can be charming and calm, and then if something doesn't go right, he loses it. He can be abusive." Current staff members confirmed for Bob what the departing people had observed.

However, the manager showed little self-awareness of his behavior and how he was perceived by his staff. Not only did he dismiss their complaints, but he actually blamed them for his behavior with such statements as, "If they did what they were supposed to, I wouldn't have to be so loud in motivating them." He used the word "loud," while his staff described the same behaviors as "temper tantrums" and "abusive." His company placed him on probation, and when the situation did not improve, they dismissed him. When he left, he accused his staff of engaging in a "witch hunt." His coping style of accusing others and denying his own role in the troubled department proved self-defeating.

A lack of self-awareness need not be associated with the kind of abusive behaviors shown by this manager. Larry, the advisor whom we described in Chapter 3, practiced the presumptive close. His main coping technique was to minimize or dismiss questions raised by his clients. We noted that, while Larry did not intend to be rude, he could easily be seen as insensitive. Very importantly, we observed that he might not even be aware of how his tone of voice and intense facial expressions supported his verbal message.

Throughout this book we've described advisors whose coping behaviors earned them the label of Charismatic Advisor, while others, such as Larry, Andrew, and Carla, wouldn't qualify for this accolade, given the counterproductive nature of their coping. As you read the following three major coping strategies displayed by clients, think about the main coping techniques that you use in both your personal and professional life and whether the way you handle difficult events is constructive or self-defeating. If they seem to be self-defeating, how do you plan to change?

The Dragon, the Ostrich, and the Owl

Human beings are a complex lot, and it stands to reason that we've all developed a multitude of coping strategies. To simplify things, we've selected three strategies that we've seen clients use repeatedly and we then offer suggestions of how Charismatic Advisors might respond to each one. We call these three the Dragon, the Ostrich, and the Owl.

The Dragon. We all know dragons in our personal and professional lives. They're quick to challenge and place others on the defensive. They tend to be angry. They may express their anger in more muted ways, such as when Ann Needham said to Todd, "Todd, you are a good talker," or in more direct ways as when a client says to an advisor, "It's your fault I'm losing so much money. You're a terrible advisor."

Dragons frequently present with a more confrontational air; remember Art Lansing, who immediately voiced reserve about seeing a financial advisor and asserted, "A friend saw a financial advisor, and he said he ended up losing money in his portfolio. Do most of your clients make money with your advice?"

It's important to keep in mind that the anger displayed by many Dragons frequently masks feelings of anxiety and vulnerability, which they have difficulty acknowledging. While it may feel more comfortable to ignore a Dragon by not returning calls, becoming angry yourself, or just not taking him on as a client, there are techniques, such as those introduced in Chapter 1, to help you decide whether a collaborative relationship can be developed before you abandon working with a Dragon.

Being aware of the Dragon's coping strategies and reaction to stress as well as your own reaction to stress may help you lessen his anger and strengthen a feeling of collaboration and resilience. Here's a possible opener to the dialogue:

"Mr. Dragon, it's natural at times for us to have differences of opinion, but it's important to work together so you feel you're actively involved and comfortable with any decisions we make. If you ever feel we're not working as closely together as you'd like, please let me know."

This statement serves several purposes. It helps lessen the Dragon's tendency to blame you for the market conditions, and it emphasizes that he's an active participant in the process. If he continues to lay blame and express anger, you can empathize — but remember that empathizing does not imply either being apologetic or being in agreement. You might say, "I know you're very angry and disappointed, but the decisions that we made were based on the best information we had at that time. A lot of people are upset in this kind of market, but you have choices. We can sit

97

down and review your portfolio to see what modifications might be in order. If after our review you still feel unsure, I'd be happy to recommend other advisors for you to interview."

Advising clients that they have a choice typically reinforces for them that they have some control over their own destiny. As we mentioned in Chapter 2, a sense of personal control is a major feature of a stress-hardy, resilient individual. If the client eventually decides to see another advisor, at least you can feel comfortable knowing that you did what you could do to create a more collaborative relationship.

The Ostrich. A major coping technique when confronted with a problematic situation is to avoid that situation. In the previous chapter we discussed "avoidance motivation." We selected the ostrich as the animal to represent avoidant behaviors for the obvious reason: the image most of us have of the ostrich is of a bird sticking its head in the sand.

In financial matters the Ostrich is the kind of client who attempts to ignore everything taking place around him. Probably, he hasn't opened his statements or checked his financial accounts in months. He no longer reads the business section of the newspaper and uses the remote control to switch quickly from any channel where discussions of the markets are taking place, and he is not likely to call his advisor to discuss his portfolio. In a paradoxical way, he maintains a sense of control through denial and cultivated ignorance.

Just as the Dragon uses anger and a confrontational approach to deal with anxiety, the Ostrich is famed for using denial. While the Dragon and the Ostrich outwardly cope differently, they are both attempting to ward off unpleasant feelings, such as anxiety, since they don't possess in their behavioral repertoire more effective techniques for managing their worries. As we mentioned earlier, it's important to recognize that while the coping behaviors of the Dragon and the Ostrich are counterproductive, they were developed for a purpose. They serve as a protective shield, and if you are to interact constructively with these clients, you must help them feel comfortable and safe with you so they will take the risk of lowering these faulty shields and approach the world in a more realistic, optimistic, resilient way.

When working with the Ostrich, you will probably have to initiate any conversation, since it's not likely the Ostrich will take this step. You also need to guard against falling into Ostrich mode yourself. In troubling times one can easily develop the Ostrich perspective: "If I don't hear from certain clients, they're probably not worried about what's occurring with their portfolio. Why cause anxiety by contacting them?" The problem is that you can't run away from reality, and a failure to confront the situation will eventually result in greater worry and frustration.

What is the best way to initiate a discussion with the Ostrich without evoking too much anxiety, which then result in greater avoidance? You might call the Ostrich, or if you think a call may be too startling, you can e-mail him and simply note that you will be calling in the next day or two to check in. Once you make the call, you might say:

"I can imagine how you must be feeling in this environment; many people share your feelings. Some people are so upset with what's going on that they can't take their eyes off business shows on TV. Other folks get very angry with others or the financial situation or even themselves. And some are so upset and worried that they don't even open their statements. But all these responses don't really help build a more secure portfolio. We haven't spoken in a while — let's schedule a time for you to come in so we can discuss your account and what's happening in the market. I think I can really help reallocate your portfolio, not only to lessen future losses but to put yourself in a favorable position when the market begins to go up."

When advisors skillfully and sensitively encourage the Ostrich to lift his head out of the sand, they will promote a more resilient posture in the Ostrich.

The Owl. We selected the image of the "wise owl" to represent the client who tends to remain calm and does not blame herself or others for the losses in her portfolio; instead, she is open to analyzing data and planning for the future. She is motivated to review her accounts in depth to find ways to take advantage of the current downturn. She will consider different portfolio allocations that would best meet her needs. She expects to hear from you, but she's not hesitant to initiate contact. While some people assume the role of the Owl easily because of their innate temperament and life experiences, we believe that advisors can assist even Dragons and Ostriches to become more Owl-like in how they approach financial uncertainty.

Given the choice, parents would love their children to have an "easy" temperament, not a "difficult" one. And if advisors had the choice, most would gravitate toward the Owls. However, this is not the reality of an advisor's life, even if we could predict what category a client will fall into. Remember that during good times many clients may appear as Owls, but they become transformed into Dragons or Ostriches when stress and pressure change their mindset and tolerance for risk.

Imagine the following ad: "I am the advisor you are seeking as long as you are cooperative, personable, reasonable, blame free, and open to advice. Others need not call. I don't want unnecessary headaches." Such an advisor might end up with few referrals and an extremely limited clientele.

A Final Thought about Coping Strategies

Early in Bob's training he was introduced to the notion of "defense mechanisms," behaviors that people used to ward off unpleasant thoughts and feelings. For Bob the term conjured up negative images — the concept suggested that people were constantly in a defensive position when trying to manage challenges in their lives, rather than assuming a more proactive stance.

As Bob adopted a strength-based approach that focused on the positive qualities of people, he was drawn to the concept of "coping strategies" in place of "defense mechanisms." This shift represented more than simply a matter of semantics for him. Rather, for Bob the word "coping" captured the reality that we all face difficult situations but we have the ability to cope with and overcome these difficulties rather than defend against them. We need not be victims of circumstances.

If we are to be Charismatic Advisors, we must identify our own coping behaviors and those of our clients so we're in a better position to replace counterproductive strategies with strategies that nurture resilience in ourselves and our clients.

Reflections

Consider the last conversation you had with a Dragon. Did you allow it to color your other interactions with clients or staff that day? Reflect upon what you might have said or done differently to have diffused the Dragon or at least your reaction to the Dragon.

How about your Ostrich clients? Have you turned some of them into "sleeping dogs" by thinking, she's not calling me so I'm not going to bother her? Can you see the danger in such an approach? Write down a list of your Ostrich clients, and schedule a meeting with each of them — the sooner the better.

CHAPTER 8

Teams in Harmony

The trend throughout the financial advisory community has been for individuals to join each other in teams, so it seems appropriate to visit this very important topic. We believe it is virtually impossible to be a Charismatic Advisor while operating within a dysfunctional team.

Recently, after having given a speech at a national conference, David was chatting with Keith, a 27-year industry veteran. "Keith, tell me about your team," David asked. Keith replied, with a bit of a twinkle in his eye, "We bring the 'fun' to dysfunctional." Funny, yet not so funny. Despite numerous extraordinary attributes that David found through further conversation with Keith, his rather glib approach to the limitations of his team are most likely holding him back from reaching his full potential.

Charismatic Advisors whom we have met who are on teams seem to enjoy harmonious work environments. We mean "harmony" from the broadest musical perspective: First, it takes a musical score (a "plan"). Second and third, it takes various voices or instruments playing their part ("roles/responsibilities") and listening intensely ("ongoing monitoring") to be certain that everything is blending well. Finally, the complete sound is almost always more significant than the sum of the parts ("synergistic").

So what makes a "team in harmony"? Almost always, there's an element of sincere collegiality. Quite simply, team members actually like one another and enjoy each other's company.

Yet there are many teams with whom we interact that like each other but are not particularly functional; our definition of functionality relates to all four of the harmonic concepts above. Ultimately though, the proof is in the pudding. When coaching teams, David typically asks the advisors, "Are you convinced that the success of your business, defined as the quality of *the client experience* and the revenue that you produce, is better than it would be if you were all operating as individuals?" In other words, is the sum truly greater than its parts?

Let's review some basic characteristics of "functionality."

A Common Vision ("Sense of Purpose")

Perhaps the most important starting point is to begin with the end in mind. Recently, David was introduced to a very substantial team, at least as measured by assets under management, on the West Coast. He gave the definition of highly functional teams and then asked the question, "On a scale of 1 to 10, with 10 being completely *firing on all cylinders* and 1 being the polar opposite, how would you rank your team?" The first five members all gave the team either 8s or 9s. The final and youngest team member said, "I would give us a 5, and that's generous!"

Well, the conversation got interesting in a hurry. What followed was a candid discussion from the youngest partner of what she felt could be improved. Eventually, the other members agreed with her and decided it was time to start by setting a higher bar for the team's sense of purpose.

Highly functional teams have taken the time to seriously consider their vision/mission/sense of purpose. They continually discuss the following kinds of questions:
- Who are we?
- Where are we trying to go?
- What are we hoping to represent in the lives of the clients we serve?
- How many clients do we want to have ultimately?
- What do we want our client experience to look like and, more importantly, to feel like?
- What is the consistency of the client experience?
- What types of clients are not a fit for our practice?
- How would we hope clients would perceive our team?
- What are the words we would hope they would use to describe us?

Not long ago, David was coaching a team and when he asked whether they had a common purpose, the following dialogue ensued:

"Yeah, we've gone through all of that 'mission stuff.'"

"Terrific, what is your sense of mission?" David asked.

The response was a bit anticlimactic: "To go from today's $3 million in revenue to $10 million within five years."

Is this a mission? Is this really a sense of purpose? This is a revenue goal. Sure, it might be part of a team's goals, but optimally, in a client-centric world the mission should be grounded elsewhere. Recall our discussion in Chapter 2 about stress hardiness and the concept of "commitment" and the need to develop a genuine purpose or higher calling to your work.

Clear Roles and Responsibilities

While vision is critical, it is not enough to capture true synergies. Often, even if a team has invested the energy to craft a powerful and client-centric mission statement, it sits on the shelf as the introduction to a yet-to-be implemented business plan or as an elegantly framed wall decoration in the conference room. The best teams we find have carefully thought through how best to allocate resources in order to actually deliver their agreed-upon sense of purpose. These teams are not teams in name only or just collections of people. They tend to think as a small business and assign roles and responsibilities to each player.

For example, does it really make sense to have everyone on a team play the role of "rainmaker"? Perhaps several players have certain strengths that can harmonize with others who have different strengths, thereby leading to higher team functionality. We selected this particular example of the rainmaker to illustrate that often the decision about roles can lead to team dysfunction and simmering discord as the most talented rainmaker may feel that others are not pulling their own weight.

Engaging in a strengths/weaknesses assessment. David has found that the best way for teams to think through decisions on the allocation of scarce team resources is to start with a classic strengths/weaknesses assessment. This involves a brainstorming session in which team members get together to discuss their sense of their own and each other's strengths and weaknesses. This typically also includes an exercise that leads to an assessment of the type of people each member of the team is "best with." The only way this exercise can be effective is if it's done with complete candor and openness. To maintain a positive and productive environment, David gets all members to promise that nothing said in the session will be held or used against any teammate.

Once the team has thoroughly discussed individual player strengths, it often becomes obvious that a restructuring is required to maximize synergistic opportunities. Weaknesses are also very important to work through. While it's sometimes possible for individuals to address their weaknesses, the most worthwhile approach can be to recognize such individual weaknesses and then do a structural "work-around" organizationally so that the identified player's weakness doesn't breed team dysfunctionality.

Let's turn to an example. David was coaching a rather large team in the Midwest that was the product of two successful teams deciding to come together. The new team consisted of six financial advisors and four staff support people. Early in the coaching process, the strengths/weaknesses discussion got underway, and it soon became clear that Frank, one of the senior partners, sat on the critical path of much of what went on in the team because of his love of detail. Frank's detail orientation was dragging down the team across virtually every core discipline.

What was Frank "best at"? It turns out the entire team believed that Frank was, by far, the most competent professional investor of the group. In fact, several of his partners were convinced that Frank was the best investor in their city. Frank had a 25-year history of trend spotting and "against the herd" risk management. Upon further reflection, the team started to appreciate that Frank had a "higher and best" use that could be far better deployed by the team. Frank could be used to differentiate the team, allowing him to focus completely on what he did best, and thereby delivering an improved and consistent client experience from an investment perspective; this plan also removed him from the day-to-day functions that were bogging the team down. Frank became the team's "Investment Committee Chair." This move created major benefits for the team from marketing to operations and, perhaps most importantly, an enhanced client experience.

A Positive Work Environment

Imagine how the environment has changed on this team. From being a perceived obstacle to the team's functioning effectively, Frank became transformed, along with the team dynamics. "It is what it is" can be a terribly self-limiting belief for teams. Often the way things are become the way things stay. Teams are like families: people can get used to their own "house noises" and never step back to assess whether there might be another way to approach things.

Many teams develop friction. You can have the best players on the planet, a common sense of mission, and clearly articulated roles and responsibilities, and still major problems can arise. Without a positive work environment, the best-laid plans can go right down the drain. No matter what the team structure (equals joined together, seasoned veteran brings in junior partner, succession-driven marriage, family partnership, lead with supporting cast) or the personalities of the players, there are skills that the Charismatic Advisor brings to the table that transcend structure and personality and lead to a positive work environment. Let's briefly explore this skill set.

Accountability. A common team ailment is a lack of accountability. Teammates get together for a planning meeting and agree upon various initiatives and in their next planning meeting discuss the same yet-to-be-accomplished initiatives. Why is this a prevalent phenomenon in our industry? We believe the central problem resides in a lack of ownership and accountability.

In an effort to maintain a collegial environment, the team takes on characteristics of a club instead of a business enterprise. Collegiality and accountability need to live in harmony for high functionality to exist.

Desire to praise and develop. In order to have high functionality, Charismatic Advisors appreciate the importance of positive reinforcement and professional development of all teammates. Both of us speak often about our observation that modern society suffers from a "praise deficit." In an ironic twist overachievers often feel the most underappreciated. It is difficult to maintain a positive work environment without ongoing encouragement and praise of those around us. People can't read minds. Sometimes we hear, "Of course Sally knows I think she is terrific!" Does she? When was the last time you told her so?

Beyond encouragement and praise, Charismatic Advisors tend to be committed to the professional development of their team-mates. Professional development can go well beyond the technical aspects of the business, given all that Charismatic Advisors have to share. Consider the example of John Waldron, who takes the role of mentoring his staff very seriously.

John Waldron, consistently high on *Barron's* Top 100 advisor rankings, leads Waldron Wealth Management in Pittsburgh. John is deeply committed to the development of his team. He sees the biggest challenge as the need to constantly remind junior team-mates to listen. In John's words, "Junior people get so excited about what they want to convey that they miss some critical client data."

John believes one of his core skills is his innate ability to know what people are going to need. He calls this "sensing." John explains: "The concept of 'need' in financial services is completely intangible. Our goal initially is to help clients actually understand what they truly need and then to describe our services so they make that connection. Teaching 'sensing' is very hard to do. I focus my teammates on working toward anticipating what the client is going to ask us."

Accurate Self-Awareness. As discussed in Chapter 7, Daniel Goleman's work on emotional intelligence (EQ) provides guidance for the Charismatic Advisor as team member. His discussion of "self-awareness" speaks to the critical importance of understanding one's own emotions and then recognizing the impact of those emotions on others. A major aspect of Bob's clinical work is helping his patients become increasingly self-aware of their feelings, thoughts, and coping strategies. When David is coaching teams, it becomes challenging when one team member's sense of his own strengths and weaknesses is not collaborated by other team members. The table below showcases examples of such potential disjointedness.

How Accurate Is Your Awareness of Yourself versus How Others See You?

See Self as	While	Others See
Driven		Abrasive
Catalytic		Manipulative
Inspirational		Dogmatic
Supportive		Condescending
Humorous		Sarcastic
Sincere		Disingenuous
Focused		Scattered
Open		Self-Centered

Develop ongoing feedback loops. Imagine the implications for an advisor who believes, for example, that he is "open," only to find that others describe him as "self-centered." If this advisor continues to think that the things he says to team members are positive ("I am just such a great, open guy"), yet each time he tells one of his stories his teammates are thinking something different ("What a self-absorbed jerk"), then the advisor doesn't even know there's a problem (not to mention the negative impact this may be causing in his client relationships!).

This necessitates building formal feedback loops into team schedules. In addition to liberally bestowing warranted praise informally (as referenced above), Charismatic Advisors on teams have carefully built formal feedback activities into their practice. But feedback loops only work if team members can be completely honest with each other without fear of repercussion.

Years ago David coached a three-person team, including two advisors and a support person who seemed to "have it all together." On a recent trip to their city, David met with them to catch up on things, only to find out that they almost "got divorced." It seems the senior partner had become very distracted by a family business his sister was running and started to materially lose focus. His junior partner could not get his attention despite continued attempts to discuss the situation, so one day he left a sealed envelope on the senior partner's desk. It contained a "notice to dissolve the partnership." This definitely got his attention! Fortunately, they brought in a mediator to help them get back on track. These two advisors had been so comfortable with each other that they relied only on informal feedback rather than building in more consistent, formal ways of providing each other with feedback. Not any more.

Empathy. We discussed empathy in some detail in Chapter 5. How does empathy relate specifically to our concept of teams in harmony? Just as empathy is a vital skill set for prospect and client interaction, it also rests at the core of teams in harmony.

Similar to the questions we posed in Chapter 5, below are a series of questions that can serve as a useful exercise for teammates to reflect upon and discuss:

- What words would you hope your team members use to describe you?
- Why are these words important to you?
- What have you said or done in the past few months to inspire your team members to use these words?
- What words would they *actually* use?
- How do you know what words they would actually use?

Another valuable set of questions that can help teams that may be experiencing some degree of friction follows:

- What experiences have you had in the past that enhanced your work environment?
- Are you incorporating those experiences into your culture today?
- How about experiences that detracted from your work environment?
- Are you avoiding or repeating these negative experiences?

Empathic Communication. This is another topic we emphasized in Chapter 5 that has much relevance for effective teaming. Sometimes in the heat of the moment, we say or do things with team-mates that we may come to regret. A difficult client encounter or paperwork snafu can have lasting scars if frustrations are taken out on teammates. Whether by instinct or deliberate practice, Charismatic Advisors use the same approach they employ with clients in their empathic communications with teammates.

Below are three important questions to keep in mind:
- Would I want anyone to say or do to me what I just said or did to a team member?
- In anything I say or do, what do I hope to accomplish?
- Am I saying things in a way that my team members are likely to hear me and not become defensive?

Let's consider the example of a family team involving a father and two sons. David was brought in by the father to determine why they weren't operating at a more effective level.

It didn't take too much time to figure out that one of the central problems of the team was that the father was critical of virtually *all* team activity. Despite repeated attempts to correct this dysfunctional reality, the sons were unable to get the father to change his ways. The conversation would usually go something like this:

Older son: "You know, Dad, my brother and I feel like you don't trust us."

Father: "Of course I trust you two! I never would have brought you both into the business if I didn't trust you. That's ridiculous."

They were very short conversations.

Let's consider this using some of the questions posed above. First, what did the older son hope to accomplish? Second, could the son have introduced the topic in a way that would have increased the probability that his father would have been more likely to *hear him* without getting defensive?

Also, could the father have responded in a way that did not shut down further discussion?

Below is an illustration of how empathic communication approaches might have gotten a better result.

Older son: "Our working together is very important to me. So I want to bring up something that may be preventing us from working as an effective team. I want to see if you sense the same thing. I feel that, in many instances, you seem to lack the trust to allow my brother and me to work independently, that you want to check all our decisions."

Note how the son used a *joining technique* by articulating the shared goal of working together, which involves focusing on an issue upon which they can agree.

Let's go back to the father for a moment.

Even though the son initially did not describe his position in a way that would likely invite ongoing dialogue, the father *still* could have used empathic communication to encourage a discussion. For example:

Father: "I'm really glad you are willing to bring this up. If we are to be an effective team, we need to be able to discuss these issues."

Note that the father used both *validation* and *joining techniques*. As we discussed in Chapter 5, validation is not necessarily agreeing but rather acknowledging — "I hear what you are saying." In this case the father does not say he agrees with his son's assessment but rather, "I'm glad you are bringing this up." This invites further discussion.

Joining involves finding something that parties agree upon that can be used as the basis of the discussion. In this case, the joining is around the mutual goal of having an effective team.

Personal control and responsibility. As highlighted in Chapter 2, Charismatic Advisors take personal control and responsibility for things that are not going right. They don't blame themselves or others for what is occurring, but they ask themselves, "What might I say or do differently to improve the situation?"

A few years ago David was asked for help from Gary, a 47-year-old advisor in Pennsylvania who had recently joined Joe, a 64-year-old advisor. This was a succession-driven marriage. Joe wanted to retire in two years, and Gary's mission was to convert Joe's clients from a transaction orientation to a planning and fee-based approach.

When David was introduced to this team, Gary was already very frustrated. He had been present at a number of meetings with Joe and Joe's clients already. The central purpose of these meetings was to engage clients in conversations about the transfer of Joe's clients to Gary and a discussion about the need to do planning. Instead, the meetings were disjointed, with Joe failing to focus, engaging clients in such topics as their last round of golf at the country club.

David's recommendation was that Gary take the initiative and propose to Joe that he handle a new round of meetings with clients on his own after Joe had set up the meetings. Gary's biggest reservation was how he could possibly sell this idea to Joe.

It worked! Here's how:

Gary: "Joe, obviously, your clients love you. Given the positive relationship you already have, when we do joint meetings I sometimes feel like a third wheel, since it's understandable that they will focus their attention on you. Given our succession arrangement, if we grow the business and increase the value that we're bringing to your clients, then they will be better off and we will as well. It would be very helpful if I had an opportunity to have a meeting with the clients by myself. Would you mind setting up a handful of meetings for me and we can give this approach a try?"

Given Gary's use of empathic communication and joining, Joe was quite receptive to meeting Gary's request. By taking personal control, rather than waiting for Joe to change, or blaming him, Gary was able to use Joe's halo effect productively. He celebrated what a great guy Joe is, joining together around his and the clients' common affection for Joe, and then moved on to discover these people for himself. This approach helped Gary position himself as someone who can add to Joe's expertise and become a different, more expanded resource.

Problem solving. Charismatic Advisors tend to perceive problems as opportunities for problem solving. Teams will always have problems; the question is how to approach their resolution.

The first step is to be able to actually identify the problem. Consider the example outlined above: did the father see *trust* as a problem? We don't think he did. So, first and foremost, if a problem is to be solved, it needs to be perceived as a problem. If teammates ask a team member to modify his behavior, but it's not perceived as a problem, nothing productive is likely to follow. Instead, they must use empathic communication.

For example, they can say, "We know you don't see what we're bringing up as a problem, but we think it may be interfering with our working as effectively as we might as a team. We really think it would be helpful to discuss it further. Also, if at any point you feel we're criticizing you, please let us know, since that is not our purpose at all. Instead, our goal is for all of us to work smoothly as a team."

This statement emphasizes the goal of bringing up a problem not perceived by the team member. It also addresses the possibility of the team member's feeling criticized and becoming defensive. Bob has found in his clinical practice that when he says to a patient, "If what I am going to say to you comes across as a criticism, please let me know," the patient is less likely to experience what Bob brings up as a criticism and less likely to become defensive.

Beyond father-son teams we see the issue of problem identification most prominently in teams where "equals" have been joined together. We're not saying that bringing equals together creates bad marriages. Quite the contrary, we see many such partnerships thriving throughout the industry. But we do notice that when problems arise in such teams the ability to actually define the problem before it escalates into a full-scale "duel of egos" rarely happens.

Below are the symptoms we find in such instances:
- Growing tension between principals
- Dissolution being considered
- Increased team member anxiety
- Team factions emerging
- "Lead dog" battle going on

A methodical approach has to be brought to problem solving to rescue such teams, starting with the recognition that both partners need to accept responsibility to change. The partners can see this as an opportunity to make the team stronger.

Often bringing in an objective facilitator can be quite useful. The best facilitators will frame their role in a way that's similar to the discussion we had surrounding advisors' roles with clients where there are problems with husbands' and wives' negative scripts:

- "It's very important for you to know that I am not here as a judge."
- "It's my responsibility to help the two of you figure out solutions that both of you will be comfortable with."

To assist the team, we can apply the "exception rule" introduced in Chapter 4 about negative scripts. In this instance, partners can be asked to consider the following questions:

- "Can you think of a problem you faced where the two of you were able to find a solution?"
- "How about a situation that you have *not* been able to resolve together?"
- "What do you see as the difference between the two situations?"
- "In what ways did you handle each of these situations differently?"
- "What do you see as each other's strongest skills?"
- "What do you see as your strongest skills?"
- "How could you apply the success you previously enjoyed and your perception of your own and each other's strongest skills to resolve the problems that you are wrestling with today?"

A Concluding Thought about Teams

Teams in *harmony* don't happen by accident; highly functional teams are created and nurtured. Perhaps most importantly, clients and prospects readily spot problems with teams. Try to see what your clients see when they come to your office for a meeting. Does the person who greets them seem to enjoy his or her job? When the meeting takes place, do the clients feel the presence of multiple minds brought to the table? Is there a sense of harmony?

Reflections

Remember "venn diagrams" from grade school, junior high, or high school? For those who may not have been exposed to venn diagrams, they comprise overlapping circles that indicate what properties or functions or responsibilities are shared and which are not. If you were to draw the venn diagram depicting your team functions, what would it look like?

For many teams, instead of modest intersects, the circles have substantial overlap, due to lack of role clarity. Such teams often are inefficient, have significant redundancies in processes, and are sometimes hampered by considerable conflict. Is there noticeable overlap in your diagram? If so, is it diminishing team functionality? Is it diminishing team harmony? What can be done to diminish the areas of intersect to improve the client experience and team efficiencies?

CHAPTER 9

Discovering Your Unique Brand: Capturing Referable Moments

Charismatic Advisors get more referrals!

Okay, you caught us. We have no statistics to back up this statement, but our experience tells us it is so. Interestingly, these advisors share two things in common. First, they get even *more* referrals during and in the aftermath of extremely difficult environments. Second, they get referrals from clients *without* having to ask for them.

Crescendo of Referable Moments

During difficult markets and in the early phases of recovery, people are thinking and talking about money — making it, losing it, keeping it. It's on the public's mind much more prominently than during good times. (As we all know, fear is often a far more powerful force than greed.) Therefore, "referable moments," opportunities your clients have to tell friends and colleagues about the value you bring to their lives and financial well-being, are occurring at a historic rate for financial advisors. The question is: *Will your clients brag about you*? *Will they use words that capture your role as a Charismatic Advisor?* If your answer is no, these precious "referable moments" will be squandered.

Let's look more closely at the issues related to referrals.

Classic Industry Training

To the financial advisory industry, referrals have always been somewhat of an obsession, involving a quandary of questions, including these:
- Whom do you ask?
- When do you ask?
- How do you ask for them?

Let's draw an analogy. If your cardiologist asked you, as a patient, to send some of your friends his way, you'd probably wonder why — why would someone you likely consider tops in the field need to ask for a referral? In many instances it would erode your sense of that doctor's quality, ability, and professionalism. It's really no different for financial advisors. People want to believe they are seeing the *best* cardiologist, and the same holds true for their financial health; they want to believe they are using the *best* financial advisor. If they believe that you are tops in your field and extremely successful, then you should be turning away prospective clients because your calendar is already very full. Asking them for referrals could severely diminish that impression.

Just to be clear, we are not discussing center-of-influence networking. Specialists in any field typically network with professionals in related fields. Cardiologists network with general practitioners. Financial advisors, for example, network with CPAs, trust and estate lawyers, and other professionals.

Advisors with mature practices who have been in the business a long time are often uncomfortable asking for referrals. We applaud them, given our cardiologist analogy. How can an advisor attract new clients without seeming like she needs the business? Affluent people, in particular, generally do not want to be "hit on" for referrals, and a direct approach often may do more harm than good.

Brandability and Referable Moments

Charismatic Advisors understand they can attract new clients without having to make a direct request. Part of this relates to the fact that these advisors serve clients at a deeper level than their "noncharismatic" colleagues. It also relates to the observation that Charismatic Advisors are simply more "brandable." So when a referable moment arises, their clients tend to describe their advisor in a way that opens up more questions from their friend.

Let's look at "brand" a bit closer. "Brand" is simply *what do you do* and *whom do you serve. Good* branding tells the story of who you are, how you're different, and why it matters. You know you have successfully defined and articulated your brand when clients describe you in an impassioned way. Those referable moments, when someone asks, "What does he/she do?" are a great opportunity for you and your firm to distinguish yourself from a branding perspective. And the way to start is by figuring out how to best make your unique "brand" stand out in the minds and on the lips of your clients. So finding the right vocabulary is vital.

How your client describes you is key and obviously can make a huge difference. Imagine that Joe and his friend are enjoying a cup of coffee in a neighborhood hangout. Advisor Alan happens to walk in and sees Joe, his client. When Alan comes over to chat, Joe introduces the friend. After Alan walks away the friend asks the typical American question, "What does Alan do?" **This is a referable moment**, and what Joe says in response, *the words he uses to describe Alan's role in his life*, can make all the difference between opening and closing the door on the friend's interest in learning more about him.

There are several things Joe might say in answering that question:
- "He's my broker."
- "He manages my money."
- "He buys stocks for me."
- "He buys bonds for me."
- "He helps me pick money managers or mutual funds."

If Joe chooses any of these run-of-the-mill, vanilla descriptions, it could well be an end to the friend's interest in hearing more about Alan. A "referable moment" has been squandered, perhaps forever.

So what words entice people to want to know more about a person? What makes you *referable?* What do your clients say about you? What would you *like* them to say?

There are some guidelines to help you choose how to best describe who you are and what you offer. For instance, steer clear of such generic words as "comprehensive" and "holistic." Avoid more formal "brochure speak" in favor of "people speak." Talk in a manner that people can easily relate to. Determine what it is that you *actually* do for people on a deeper level — what do you represent in their minds and hearts?

Advisors with a strong sense of their role and purpose tend to have an easier job of defining "what they do" in a more impassioned way. An advisor who built a very powerful brand did so because of the compelling way in which he positioned himself and his personal message. He began the thought process to define his brand by reviewing the kind of relationships he wanted to build with his clients. His positioning sounds like this: ". . . from the beginning, I explain that my goal is to become an integral part of their big life decisions. To do that, I need to become a part of the fabric of their lives. While I make it clear that I don't expect to come to dinner every week, I let them know that I plan on having a metaphorical seat at their table."

Ultimately, positioning and passion statements can help advisors discover their unique brand.

To work well and be effective, your brand should
- Be from the gut — it should resonate with people;
- Be brief, forceful, and meaningful in expression;
- Actually *fit what you do*, not be a descriptor you adopted from someone else;
- Most importantly, use words that flow easily no matter who is using them — you, your colleagues, your family, and, most especially, your clients.

The second part in creating a powerful brand focuses on the notion of **whom you serve** — who is your optimal target audience, who are the clients you want to reach? You should consider a number of important common denominators in getting to the "who":
- Gender
- Age
- Occupation
- Stage of life
- How they came into their money
- Needs
- How they make decisions

You want to stand apart from your competitors, but don't think solely about demographics. What *special* needs do you meet that make you unique? For example, the brand David helped one advisor create explicitly references that he specializes in providing financial services to widows.

We help widows deal with the unique challenges they confront when it comes to money.

Remember Todd Silaika, our Charismatic Advisor whose letter to his clients we reprinted in Chapter 4? He and his partners, Erick Richardson and Scott Calhoun, have an extremely pithy brand that resonates perfectly with their target clients: "We deliver *worry-free retirement* for people retiring from corporate America."

Developing your unique brand may not be easy, but it can very well be the most important step you take in getting more referrals. Let's return to our earlier example. The cardiologist analogy actually comes from interactions David has had with his cardiologist, Dr. Gladys. What if, instead of asking for a referral, the doctor had "branded" herself by expressing her capabilities and specialties, qualifying who her patients are, what she does for them specifically, and why she cares about them? She could say, "You know, I'm glad you came to me because I specialize in preventive cardiology for very active, middle-aged people like you, David, who may have family history or high cholesterol. I don't want to worry that you may be having chest pains on the mountain trails when you're biking with your buddies."

The cardiologist is "branding" herself and, in doing so, making it easy for patients to share her professional qualities and personal attributes with others. Next time David is biking with his friends and someone complains about "feeling a strange pain" lately, he will instinctively respond, "You should see Dr. Gladys. She specializes in guys like us."

The "brand" succeeds in capturing the doctor's specialty and her audience. Did she plant a seed as to how and whom David should refer to her? Absolutely. Did she ask him for a referral? Absolutely not.

Branding, if done well, should be designed to achieve consistency and express what sets you apart from your competitors. Creating a brand that establishes your significant, distinctive presence in the market can attract — and retain — loyal clients. Your brand should capture your specific higher calling.

Dig Deep

Charismatic Advisors approach this effort seriously and work to bring their uniqueness to the surface. Who are you, and why should that matter to me? What makes you special?

Let's consider James Olson, an advisor from Portland, Maine, to whom David was introduced recently. James had already clearly established himself as a rising star, and as David began to get to know James, he heard things that convinced him James is destined for major success in this business. James brings a robust as well as a unique background and skill set to this business. James's biggest perceived limitation was that he has only been in the business for two years. Upon discussion, James appreciated that he needed to let go of this self-limiting belief and focus on what he brings to the table that is special.

After some coaching sessions James has completely transformed his first meeting with prospects by embracing his passions and uniqueness.

First, he doesn't offer a commercial for himself initially but spends 45 minutes fully getting to understand the client. Then he says something like the following:

> I appreciate your candor in telling me about yourself and family. It is very important for me to understand these details so that I may best determine whether we may be good partners. In the same vein, I would like to tell you a bit more about myself so that you may determine whether I might be a good fit for you.
>
> There are several primary features of my past that have had the most significant impact on who I am and how I do business. The first of these is related to my upbringing. As a child, I was not the beneficiary of many of the elements that the "great American family" enjoys. I was required, to a significant degree, to find my own way. I believe that, ultimately, this left me extremely interested and sensitive to people's life experiences. It also made me appreciate the value of earning trust rather than simply asking for it. I say this to you because I recognize the gravity of being entrusted with the wealth and ultimately the hopes and dreams of my clients.
>
> My humble beginnings also instilled in me a disciplined work ethic. I had to work extremely hard to create opportunities for future growth and prosperity for myself and my family.

Another important component of my past is my history as a competitive athlete. I competed in collegiate basketball, rowing, track and field and, later, as a competitive cyclist. I was not a natural or particularly gifted athlete as a child. Yet I found success by being committed and disciplined. I believe that my competitive nature is a valuable attribute. I am driven to succeed because I do not like to see my clients lose.

Finally, my experience as a material scientist and semiconductor device physicist may be one of my most useful attributes. I was awarded over 20 international patents and have published technical articles in numerous journals and textbooks based on my success in solving problems.

In short, I recognize the value of trust, the importance of discipline, commitment and structure.

Find Your Passion

You may recall that we discussed the notion of seeking a higher calling in Chapter 2. Charismatic Advisors tend to have identified their passion and know how to channel it into their approach to client interaction. Here are a few examples from advisors previously mentioned.

Remember John Rafal of Essex Financial? John's found his "higher calling," and it goes far beyond helping his clients financially. John has a passion for helping people through life's events and is especially present in the difficult moments. Years ago John told David a story about a client's son who had gotten into some potentially serious trouble. The lawyer the client had selected was not helping, so John immediately stepped in and found the client a more appropriate attorney for the predicament, and ultimately, the story had a happy ending.

As John points out, "What matters is all the little things you do for your clients. I spend a lot of time on how they feel about where they are in their life. You must be consistent. It takes a lot of time, but it is my passion for this business."

We discussed Augie Cenname earlier in the book. Years ago, Augie had a near-death experience in a horrific auto accident. The positive attitude that emerged for him from the accident was the notion that you never know what life has in store for you. He took away the conviction that you must live every moment of your life in the present. David once asked him over lunch, "You seem so focused on our conversation and have this remarkable ability to have me feel like nothing is more important to you in the world than speaking to me right now. How do you do it?"

Augie replied, "Because nothing *is* more important. How do I know this won't be the last conversation of my life? We could leave this restaurant and I could cross the street and get hit by a bus. My passion has become to live every moment to the fullest. I bring this passion to every client interaction."

Concluding Thoughts

Charismatic Advisors identify their passion and then channel that passion into their client conversations and their unique brand. Ultimately, the Charismatic Advisor lives in the conversations between advisor and prospect, advisor and client, and advisors' clients with their friends and family when the advisor is not even in the room. Find your passion and bring it into your practice. In the next chapter we turn to the legacy of the Charismatic Advisor.

Reflections

You already have a brand — your clients see you in a certain light. In considering your brand, think about the following questions:

- How would I like my clients to describe me in a referable moment?
- What do I say and do that will lead them to describe me in this way?
- How would they actually describe me?
- Do I actively seek their feedback so I know how they would describe me?
- What steps must I take if there is a noticeable discrepancy between the way I hope they would describe me and the words they would actually use to describe me?

Years ago, Nate Winstanley, a dear friend of David from Lenox, Massachusetts, taught him the expression, "Better to be discovered than announced." It is a powerful notion. Do you work aggressively to attract new clients, or do you focus on becoming attractive to those you would like most to serve? This question expressly relates to your brand.

Anchoring much of David's advisor-coaching activities is the word "purposeful." Advisors interested in capturing referable moments seek to discover the appropriate vocabulary that best fits their unique passion and approach. But far beyond words, such advisors make certain that their day-to-day conversations and ongoing processes align with the chosen description. A "brand" must live consistently in the actual client experience that's delivered. "Purposeful" behavior optimally relates to deep reflection and an understanding of one's purpose and where one fits in the life of a client.

CHAPTER 10

The Legacy of the Charismatic Advisor

In considering the format and content of this final chapter, we agreed that we didn't want to use it to summarize each chapter of the book. Instead, we reflected upon the many questions we posed throughout the book, especially those related to how we are seen by our clients and how we would like to be seen and what role we play in their lives.

We kept returning to the word "legacy," questioning, "What is it that we wish to leave others in any of our personal or professional activities?" Bob, in his writings about resilience in children, has often asked, "What is the legacy we want to impart to our children?" He has answered in part, "Not just a financial inheritance but deep-rooted gifts such as values, moral standards, love, compassion, hope, and resilience."

We believe that Charismatic Advisors provide an invaluable legacy for their clients, as well as for the children and grandchildren of their clients. Certainly, financial security is involved. However, if your clients were to describe you and the important role you have played in their lives, we would guess that, in addition to mentioning that you helped to craft and implement a financial plan, you would hope they add other descriptions. What would you like these descriptions to include?

As we thought about the question of legacy, we considered the words of Ralph Waldo Emerson. Emerson grappled with the question of what composes a successful life. He wrote the following description:

> To laugh often and much;
> To win the respect of intelligent people and the affection of children;
> To earn the appreciation of honest critics and endure the betrayal of false friends;
> To appreciate beauty, to find the best in others;
> To leave the world a bit better, whether by a healthy child, a garden patch or a redeemed social condition;

To know even one life has breathed easier because you have lived.

This is to have succeeded.

In specifically targeting the legacy of Charismatic Advisors, we would like to add the following to Emerson's reflections:

To contribute to the financial security of our clients;

To help our clients discover how money fits into their lives;

To encourage our clients to assume personal control of their lives and become proactive in making sound decisions;

To help our clients identify and live life in concert with their values;

To assist our clients in finding ways to have the time and flexibility to follow their interests and passions;

To lessen the burdens and worries of our clients so they have more time and energy to focus on nurturing their relationships with family and friends.

Please feel free to add to this list.

As we end this chapter, we wish to emphasize another point. If we, as Charismatic Advisors, leave for our clients the kind of legacy we have outlined above, in the process we will also enrich our own lives and the lives of our families. Our legacy will indeed reach many people and be long lasting.

It is our hope that this book will serve as an important resource, one to which you will return on many occasions as you strive to be a Charismatic Advisor who will leave a legacy of inestimable value to those whose lives you have touched.